Religious Cults Associated With the Amazons

By

Florence Mary Bennett

First published in 1912

Published by Left of Brain Books

Copyright © 2023 Left of Brain Books

ISBN 978-1-397-66886-8

First Edition

All rights reserved. No part of this publication may be reproduced, distributed, or transmitted in any form or by any means, including photocopying, recording, or other electronic or mechanical methods, without the prior written permission of the publisher, except in the case of brief quotations permitted by copyright law. Left of Brain Books is a division of Left Of Brain Onboarding Pty Ltd.

PUBLISHER'S PREFACE

About the Book

"Bennett's thesis explores the possible religious beliefs of the Amazons. She examines the legend of the Amazons and many of the goddess cults of ancient Greece and Asia Minor (Turkey). Her research is, as befits a scholarly paper, extensively documented. The footnote to text ratio is extremely rich.

Bennett describes in great detail what is known about ancient goddess worship through primary documents. She describes many details that are taken for granted today, such as the double axe symbol, and some aspects that are not so well understood. For instance, some of the male deities of later classical Greek religion turn out to originally be of ambiguous gender. And Aphrodite, who in later mythology is a love goddess, was originally a war goddess.

Whether or not the Amazons were literal history or belonged to the realm of pure mythology, they left an indisputably huge trace in classical literature. This monograph is a superb summation of this evidence."

(Quote from sacred-texts.com)

CONTENTS

PUBLISHER'S PREFACE
   THE AMAZONS IN GREEK LEGEND 1
   THE GREAT MOTHER 14
   EPHESIAN ARTEMIS 24
   ARTEMIS ASTRATEIA AND APOLLO AMAZONIUS 32
   ARES 47
CONCLUSION 60
BIBLIOGRAPHY 64
ENDNOTES 70

＃ THE AMAZONS IN GREEK LEGEND

THE Iliad contains two direct references to the Amazons:-- namely, in the story of Bellerophon[1] and in a passage from the famous teichoscopy.[2] The context to which the first of these belongs is classed by critics as an "echo" from the pre-Homeric saga, and therefore it may be inferred that the Amazon tradition in Greek literature dates from a time even earlier than the Homeric poems. The description of the women here is very slight, being given by the epithet ἀντιανείρας of the line τὸ τρίτον αὖ' κατέπεφνεν Ἀμαζόνας ἀντιανείρας,[3] but, from the facts that battle with them is considered a severe test of the hero's valour and that as warriors they are ranked with the monstrous chimaera, the fierce Solymi, and picked men of Lycia, we gather that they are conceived as beings to be feared. The scene of combat with them is Lycia. The second of the two passages cited above is more definite. Priam, exclaiming on the happy lot of Agamemnon, who has been pointed out to him, says to Helen: "Oh, happy Atreïd, fate's child, blessed with prosperity! Verily, to thee are many subject, youths of the Achaeans! Once did I go to vine-rich Phrygia, where I beheld vast numbers of Phrygian men with swift-moving steeds, the people of Otreus and godlike Mygdon, who were then encamped by the banks of the Sangarius. For I was numbered an ally with these on that day when the Amazons came, pitted against men. Yet even these were not as many as are the quick-glancing Achaeans." Although the characterisation is the same as in the Bellerophon story (Ἀμαζόνες ἀντιάνειραι), there is gain in that the impression of the Amazons as a mighty band of warriors is strengthened, also that the event has its place in the conventional chronology of Greek legend, antedating the Trojan

War. It is to be noted, moreover, that here the Amazons are the aggressors on the confines of Phrygia.

There is another allusion in Homer to the Amazons, although this is indirect rather than direct. It occurs in the second book of the Iliad, where the spot of assembly for the Trojans and their allies is designated:[4] "There is before the city a certain lofty barrow, in the plain far away, standing detached on this side and on that, which men, forsooth, call Batieia, but the immortals name it the grave of swift-bounding Myrina. Here then were the Trojans numbered and their allies." The scholiast and the commentary of Eustatius on the passage tell that this Myrina was an Amazon, the daughter of Teucer and the wife of Dardanus, and that from her the city Myrina in Aeolis was said to have been named.[5] It seems reasonable to suppose that the commentators are correct, for in later literature we hear much of an Amazon by this name, and there is frequent mention of graves of various Amazons, here and there in Greek lands, always regarded with wonder and awe akin to the reverence with which Homer mentions the tomb of Myrina.

The Amazons then, as they appear in the Homeric poems, are a horde of warrior women who strive against men, and with whom conflict is dangerous even to the bravest of heroes. They belong to Asia Minor, seemingly at home in the neighbourhood of Lycia and opponents of the Phrygians on the river Sangarius About the grave of one of their number there lurks a hint of the supernatural. The poet does not say whether she was friend or foe of Troy. On the analogy of similar graves pointed out in various parts of Greece, she who lay buried there may well have been a foe, yet later Greek commentators saw in this one an ancestress of the royal line of Troy.

In this they may have drawn on the Aethiopis, which tells of an alliance between Amazons and Trojans. We pass thus from the

Homeric Epic to the Epic Cycle. Proclus in the Χρηστομάθεια Γραμματική, whence Photius quotes excerpts, says that the last book of the Iliad was followed by the Aethiopis in five books, written by Arctinus of Miletus (circa 750 B.C.). He starts the argument thus: "The Amazon Penthesilea, daughter of Ares, a Thracian by birth, appears to give aid to the Trojans. In the pride of her valour Achilles slays her, and the Trojans bury her. Achilles destroys Thersites for speaking slander against him and carping at his alleged love for Penthesilea; whence there is a division among the Greeks in regard to the murder of Thersites." It is not possible to trace the story of Penthesilea beyond the date of the Aethiopis. How much the poet made of the romantic situation drily described by Proclus, it cannot be determined, for the evidence has perished with the work. Certainly it did not lose in pathetic details at the bands of the writers and painters of later years. The outline preserved by Proclus speaks only of the "alleged love" of Achilles for the queen, yet that affords a starting-point for the play of much romantic fancy in subsequent times.[6] The fact that in the Aethiopis Penthesilea is called a Thracian raises the question whether the author does this lightly, or whether he has serious thought of Thrace as the home of the race and of Ares as their patron deity. Diodorus[7] gives Ares as the father of Penthesilea and Otrere as her mother, and St. Basil[8] adds that she was queen of the Amazons of Alope in Pontus, but elsewhere[9] Otrere too is called a daughter of Ares, her mother being Harmonia, while her children are Hippolyta and Penthesilea. Ares, however, is quite steadily named by Greek writers as the father of the Amazons in general, and Harmonia, as their mother.[10]

Another Amazon is mentioned by name in an epic fragment preserved by the scholiast on Pindar's third Nemean Ode, line 64: "Telamon of insatiate battle-shout was the first to bring light to our comrades by slaying man-destroying, blameless Melanippe, own sister to the golden-girdled queen." This new character is attested an Amazon by the epithet ἀνδρολέτειραν, a vigorous variant on ἀντιάνειρα, and by her kinship with the "golden-girdled queen," who can be none other than Hippolyta. The adjective ἀμώμητον is conventional and colourless. The fragment must belong to a long passage--if not to a whole poem--descriptive of the combat waged by Telamon and his comrades against the Amazons. [11]

That the well-worn story of Heracles and the "golden-girdled queen" had its place in some song of the Epic Cycle seems a reasonable admission, [12] and it may therefore be considered proper to sketch its simple outline, as it appears in later poetry and prose. By the excellent testimony of the early vases which show Heracles and the Amazon together the epic source of the later versions of the tale is dated in the period from the eighth to the sixth century B.C. The general plot is this:--Heracles, arrived at Themiscyra, prepares to give battle for the girdle, in search of which he has been sent, but succeeds in obtaining it from the queen without force of arms, whereupon Hera arouses the other Amazons against him. In the fight which ensues Heracles is victorious, but he slays Hippolyta. [13] For the first time we hear of Themiscyra on the Thermodon as the home-city of the Amazons. As in the case of Penthesilea and Achilles this legend of Heracles and Hippolyta has a touch of romance.

Even more romantic interest gathers about the story of Theseus and his Amazon, called usually Antiope, but often Hippolyta. The secret of this lies probably in the great vogue accorded to the traditional adventures of Theseus, the national hero of Athens. As in vase painting Heracles, once popular with the masters of the old style, was gradually crowded aside by Theseus, so it happened in literature. It would seem that the epic from which the story of Theseus and Antiope [14] was derived was later than that which was the source of the tale of Heracles, for Theseus appears in company with the Amazons only on vases of the red-figured technique, never on the older specimens of ceramic art. [15] According to Pausanias [16] there were two versions of the story of Antiope: that of Pindar, who told that she was stolen by Pirithoüs and Theseus, and that of Agias or Hegias of Troezen, who told that when Heracles with Theseus as a companion was besieging Themiscyra, Antiope betrayed the city for love of Theseus. The Athenian story of the invasion of Attica by the Amazons in search of their queen complements either version. How much material Euripides drew from the Cycle for his conception of the mother of Hippolytus as the discarded wife of Theseus cannot be determined.

The contribution which the Epic Cycle seems to have made to the idea of the Amazons presented by Homer may be summed up as characterisation of individuals of the race. To Homer the Amazons are merely a horde of redoubtable warriors, who appear at the gates of the Asiatic world. To the later epic they are a people who dwell in a city on the Euxine at the mouth of the Thermodon. They are thus conceived as a settled race on the outskirts of civilisation. They belong to the eastern lands whither only adventurers and hardy colonists dared to sail. The stories told of their heroines, Penthesilea, Hippolyta, and Antiope, bring the race into direct contact with Greek legendary history.

To say that in Homer the Amazons are creatures of fable, in the Cycle women of romantic legend, and to the Greek historians a race of the barbarians, seems a more or less serviceable way of expressing the growth of thought on this subject, so far as it is now to be ascertained. The value of such a statement lies in its being suggestive, rather than strictly accurate in detail. It is only another way of saying that epic verse as a medium of narration had given place to prose. Evidently the invasion of Attica, an event probably first described in the Cycle, is the historic fact, as the Greek historians regarded it, on which all doubts about the reality of the Amazons [17] might be broken, for as a memorial there were to be seen many tombs of these women in Greek lands. [18] The tale which Pausanias [19] heard about the Hippolyta who was buried at Megara is probably typical of the poetic legends current among the country-folk wherever there was the tradition of the Amazons' coming:--"I will write her story as the Megarians tell it: When the Amazons made their expedition for Antiope's sake and were overcome by Theseus, it was the fate of the many to die in battle, but Hippolyta, who was sister to Antiope and was at that time in command of the women, fled with a few to Megara. But, inasmuch as she had fared so ill with her armament, and was cast down by the circumstances of the present, and was still more discouraged about a safe return to Themiscyra, she died of grief, and the shape of her tomb is like to an Amazonian shield." The place given to the invasion of the Amazons in the chronicles of the historians seems to have been as fixed as that of the Trojan War. Herodotus [20] represents the Athenians claiming a post of honour before the battle of Plataea, supporting their plea by these "deeds of eld"' (τὰ παλαιά): first, their succour of the Heraclidae, second, their campaign against Thebes in vengeance of the dead followers of Polynices, third, their courage in the face of the invaders, "who, coming from the river Thermodon, fell once upon the Attic land," and, finally, their inferiority to none in the Trojan War. The order of events here places this invasion before the Trojan War, a chronological arrangement in accord with the traditional date of Theseus.

Herodotus, it will be observed, keeps to the geographical theory of the Cycle, placing the home of these warriors on the banks of the Thermodon. Strabo [21] clearly follows Herodotus and his successors, for he calls the plain about Themiscyra τὸ τῶν Ἀμαζόνων πεδίον, but Diodorus,[22] giving the account of Dionysius of Mitylene, who, on his part, drew on Thymoetas,[23] states that a great horde of Amazons under Queen Myrina started from Libya, passed through Egypt and Syria, and stopped at the Caïcus in Aeolis, near which they founded several cities. Later, he says, they established Mitylene a little way beyond the Caïcus.

In addition to Myrina in Aeolis[24] and Mitylene on Lesbos, several cities of Asia Minor boasted that they were founded by the Amazons.[25] Consistent with these claims is the fact that in this neighbourhood the figure or head of an Amazon was in vogue as a coin-type,[26] and it is to be noted that such devices are very rarely found on coins elsewhere. In a fragment of Ephorus, who was a native of Cyme and, therefore, presumably conversant with the details of the legends thereabouts, the Amazons are said to have lived in and near Mysia, Caria, and Lydia. This evidence as a whole seems to point, not to the plain at the mouth of the Thermodon as the traditional dwelling-place of the race, but to a centre much further west, namely, to that part of Asia Minor which borders on the Aegean. It is easy too reconcile this with the geographical setting of the story of Bellerophon, wherein Homer tells that the Amazons were sought and found somewhere near Lycia. Not far away are the Island of Patmos, where there was a place called Amazonium,[27] and the island of Lemnos, where there was another Myrina.[28] Arctinus is said[29] to have introduced into the saga the motive of a cavalry combat waged by the Lydians and Magnesians against the Amazons, of which the scene would naturally be in this part of the world, but this same writer's statement, that Penthesilea, who came to the help of Troy, was a Thracian, directs the attention away from Asia Minor,[30] although Thrace lay just across the Hellespont, near the Troad. It may well be, however, that the thought of Thrace in intimate association with this queen is rather to be aligned with the facts indicating yet a third traditional home for the race, namely, in the regions of Scythia north of the Euxine and Lake Maeotis.

Herodotus evidently considered Themiscyra, the original home of the Amazons.[31] At any rate, having once designated them the "women from the Thermodon," he does not go back of the characterisation in search of their antecedents. Perhaps the service which he does perform is of greater value, in that, by pointing out a group of people whom he believes to be descended from the Amazons, he seems to be pushing these forebears of the legendary time into the full light of history. He tells[32] of the migration of a band of Amazons into the wild northern region between the Black Sea and the Caspian, beyond Lake Maeotis and the Tanaïs. From their intermarriage with the Scythians the Sauromatae were descended, a Scythian tribe among whom the women were warriors and hunters. Other writers[33] also speak of the Amazons on the Maeotic Lake, a sheet of water best known to the Greeks by its western boundary, the Tauric Chersonese, the place where Iphigeneia lived as priestess of the cruel goddess. Even the Caucasus mountains and the hazily conceived Colchian land lay nearer to the Hellenic world than this savage Scythian region. Greek travellers brought back accounts of strange customs among these northern tribes. They told of the Tauri, that they immolated all shipwrecked strangers to their Artemis,[34] and of the Sauromatae, that none of their women married until she had slain a man of the enemy,[35] The Greek equivalent, ἀνδροκτόνοι, which Herodotus gives for the Scythian word meaning "Amazon" (οἰόρπατα), is strongly suggestive of the epithets, ἀντιάνειραι and ἀνδρολέτειραι, used of the Amazons.[36]

Aeschylus in the Prometheus Bound[37] also associates the Amazons with the north. The geography of this passage is interesting in comparison with that of Herodotus, because the poet antedates the historian and therefore represents the vague reports of these regions which preceded the carefully considered mapping evolved by Herodotus. Aeschylus places the Nomad Scythians far to the north, near the Ocean, in which Strabo[38] follows him, whereas Herodotus[39] finds them definitely established on the Gulf of Carcinitis, west of the Tauric Chersonese. The Chalybes, whom Herodotus[40] and Strabo[41] locate south of the Black Sea, are by Aeschylus relegated to northern Scythia. And, strangest of all, he seems to place Mount Caucasus north of the Black Sea and the Sea of Azov. South of this are "the Amazons, man-hating, who will in a later time dwell in Themiscyra by the Thermodon." Elsewhere in the Prometheus[42] the Amazons are called "the dwellers in the Colchian land, maidens fearless in battle," and their home is evidently placed near that of "the throng of Scythia, who possess the land at the ends of the earth about Lake Maeotis." In the Suppliants[43] Aeschylus speaks again of the Amazons, here as τὰς ἀνάνδρους κρεοβόρους τ' Ἀμαζόνας, a characterisation which suggests another line of his, quoted by Strabo:[44] ἀλλ' ἱππάκης βρωτῆρες εὔνομοι Σκύθαι. Aeschylus then apparently places the original home of the Amazons in the country about Lake Maeotis, conceiving this region to be practically identical with the Colchian land, or contiguous to it. He speaks of their migrating thence to Themiscyra, while Herodotus holds the opposite theory, that they migrated from an original home at Themiscyra to Scythia. It seems proper to give the preference to the latter as the view commonly held in antiquity, for Herodotus is the later writer and the more scientific student of geography. Strabo, who had large opportunities for the comparison of conflicting accounts, pointedly says[45] that Themiscyra, the plain thereabouts, and the overhanging mountains belonged to the Amazons, and that they were driven from this home.[46]

It may be concluded that there were three centres to which Greek tradition assigned the Amazons:--one in western Asia Minor,--a large district in the form of a strip stretching from the Propontis to the tip of Lycia; the second in Pontus along the Euxine, with a western boundary at Sinope, an eastern at Colchis, and a southern undefined, somewhere in the interior of Cappadocia; a third in Scythia, conceived as the Tauric Chersonese, the regions east of Lake Maeotis, those north of the same lake, and probably also those which border the Euxine on the north and west, including Thrace. Each of these is an area so large that only by extension of the term may it be denoted a centre. Threads of affiliation reach out also to Libya, Egypt, and Syria. Out of this maze the source of the Amazon legend is to be sought. To round out this brief summary of the geography of the legend the list should be set down of the places in Greece proper which are especially mentioned in the tale of the invasion of the Amazons:--Athens,[47] Troezen,[48] Megara,[49] Chaeronea,[50] Chalcis in Euboea,[51] Thessaly.[52]

But the story of the Amazons as the Greeks thought of them would not be complete without several additional details. Among these is the tradition, which has seized powerfully on the imagination of later times, that it was the custom of these women to burn out the right breast, in order that they might the better draw the bow.[53] The story is usually explained as an attempt to derive the word Ἀμαζών, from μαζός with prefix of ἁ privative. It seems probable that this false etymology grew out of the theory that the Sarmatians were descendants of the Amazons, for Hippocrates of Cos, a younger contemporary of Herodotus, gives a detailed account of the practice among the Sarmatian women.[54] Philostratus[55] takes pains to say that the Amazons were not thus mutilated. Most cogent as an argument against the universality of the theory in ancient times is the fact that nowhere among the extant remains of Greek art is there a representation of a single-breasted Amazon. All that can be brought forward for the other side from artistic sources is that there was evidently a convention in favour of showing one breast bare in plastic and pictorial delineations of these women.

This naturally introduces the general subject of the treatment of the Amazons in Greek art. The battle between Greeks and Amazons was a favourite theme with the sculptors of friezes. Its companion pieces are the fight between Lapiths and Centaurs and the historic struggle between Greeks and Persians. In each of these subjects the Greek requisite of simplicity in art demanded that the essential element should be sought by analysis, in order that the composition might present the situation in a telling manner. It follows that the point brought out in the scenes from the Persian Wars is that Greek is pitted against Persian, in the Centauromachy, that it is civilised man against bestial man, in the conflict with the Amazons, that the battle is between man and woman. Therefore the Greek artist emphasises, in the first, the national dress of the combatants, in the second, the savage appearance of the monsters, in the third, the womanhood of the Amazons contrasted with the manhood of their enemies. Uniformly in the friezes the Amazons are beautiful. Those who have fallen are treated by the artist with peculiar tenderness; those who are brought to bay are spirited and valiant, but also delicate and frail; those who are for the moment victorious Show no savage exultation, as do the fierce Centaurs in the same situation. Their costume is usually a short tunic girt up for action, frequently open at one side in order to display the woman's figure. The effort is always, not to show them to be foreigners who wear a fantastic garb, but to indicate plainly that they are women warring with men.

The famous free-standing statues of Amazons which have come down to us, and which inherit the artistic tradition of the masters of the fifth century,[56] show the same sympathetic treatment. The face is calm and ideally beautiful, the body is that of a young woman in her prime, strong, supple, and graceful, dressed in a short tunic which leaves one breast bare.[57]

There are also examples of the mounted Amazon in sculpture. Perhaps one of the finest bits in existence is the fragment of horse and woman-rider from Epidaurus, now in the National Museum at Athens. This Amazon wears a short belted tunic and also a mantle fastened about her neck. She is remarkably lithe and beautiful; she sits her horse perfectly; best of all is the contrast between her slender body and the powerful and sinewy frame of the animal.

In the museum at Naples there is a piece of sculpture in the style of a later period. It represents a dead Amazon, lying supine. She wears the conventional dress, the short tunic which reveals the bare breast, and under her is a spear. Her lips are open in the last struggle for breath. About the whole figure there is a note of sadness. The distended breasts suggest maternity, a detail which possibly indicates that the figure of a baby was originally grouped with this Amazon. Special interest attaches to this work as a type of the Amazon in the last days of Greek art, before its vigour had departed, for it is doubtless a detail, in close copy of the original, from the group which Attalus set up on the Acropolis at Athens.[58]

In vase-paintings, rather than in sculpture, we find the characteristic weapons of the Amazons, the shield shaped like an ivy-leaf,[59] the Scythian bow,[60] and the battle-axe.[61] Here also we see the mantle of panther's skin similar to that which Penthesilea wore in the painting by Polygnotus at Delphi.[62]

The types of Amazons in vase-painting are numerous. They are shown in every conceivable situation indicative of their prowess in battle and in the hunt,--on foot, on horseback, in chariots, preparing for combat, taking the ephebes' oath, bearing away the dead, and so on. [63] The groups on the vases frequently recall the friezes. In addition to these portrayals of the Amazons in general the vases show scenes from the Heracles saga and from the legend of Theseus.

The inference is inevitable, that among the great painters the Amazons were popular as a subject, for it is to be presumed that in these themes, as in others, the potters' workshops merely followed the fashion of the art which they distantly reflected. First-hand evidence of the manner in which. painters managed the presentation is not available. The vases furnish the best information on this point, and their testimony may be eked out by a few passages from literature. [64]

Such then in a general way is the tradition of the Amazons, which had an important place in Greek art and literature. This review is the natural introduction to the study of cults associated with these women, for without a clear understanding of the legend certain details of cult-practice are obscure. The points which should bear emphasis are these:--the persistent belief among the Greeks in the real existence of Amazons; the conception of them as unusually fierce warriors, and this in spite of various tendencies of thought destructive of such an idea; the habit of associating them with certain definite geographical centres.

THE GREAT MOTHER

MORE primitive than the worship of the gods under anthropomorphic form is the custom of reverencing this or that deity in baetylic or aniconic shape, a habit of religious cult for which there is ample evidence in the writings and monuments of the Greeks. This evidence, however, usually indicates such worship only in very early times, showing that it gave place here and there to a more highly developed stage, that of iconic symbolism, but there are examples of this primitive conception of deity in late times. Conspicuous among these survivals is the worship of Cybele under the form of the Black Stone of Pessinus in Phrygia. By order of the Sibylline books the cult was transplanted to Rome, in 204 B.C., as a means of driving Hannibal out of Italy. [65]

Apollonius [66] represents the Amazons engaged in ritual exactly similar to that of Pessinus--venerating a black stone placed on an altar in an open temple situated on an island off the coast of Colchis. The character of the worship which he depicts makes it probable that he drew his information on this point from an early source, especially since we learn from Diodorus [67] that the Amazons paid marked honour to the Mother of the Gods, consecrating to her the island of Samothrace, setting up her altars there, and performing magnificent sacrifices. At any rate, the two passages substantiate the fact that the Amazons were votaries of the Mother, who was known both as Rhea and as Cybele.

One story [68] told that Scamander introduced the rites of the Cretan Mother into Phrygia, and that they were firmly established at Pessinus on the Sangarius as a chief centre, where the goddess received from the mountain ridge overhanging the city the well-known name, Dindymene; [69] another account [70] had it that the home of Phrygian Cybele's worship was in Samothrace, whence Dardanus brought the cult to Phrygia; an attempt to rationalise the two legends developed the tale [71] that Corybas of Samothrace, son of Demeter and Jasion, introduced the rites of his mother into Phrygia, and that his successors, the Corybantes of Mount Ida in the Troad, passed over to the Cretan mountain of the same name, in order to educate the infant Zeus. In the minds of the various writers of antiquity to whom we are indebted for all that we know about orgiastic cults there is such confusion that we are left in ignorance of accurate details which would serve to distinguish sharply one cult from another.

We are informed on several points, however, concerning the worship of Cybele, the Great Mother of Phrygia, considered apart from other cults similar in character and expression. Her worship at Pessinus in particular is most important to an inquiry concerning the Amazons, because there, attested by history, was the same baetylic form of the goddess under which the Amazons were said to have venerated her. Roman writers naturally, after the Black Stone had been set up in their city, were moved by interest and curiosity to examine the legends connected with the cult, and so it happens that to these sources we owe many facts, often gleaned from the poets of the early Empire who looked with disgust on the great vogue of this orgiastic cult in their day. Cybele of Pessinus was served by eunuch priests called Galli. [72] This office of priesthood, which was considered very honourable, seems to have commemorated the devotion of Atys to the goddess. Fortunately we have a record [73] of the peculiar form which the legend of Atys assumed at Pessinus. Here he was regarded as the son of a maiden by the fruit of an almond-tree, which sprang from the bi-sexual Agdistis. Agdistis [74] loved him and made him her paredros and Gallus. From the same source, Pausanias, we learn the Lydian variant of the story. [75] In this he is called the son of Calaüs of Phrygia. He established the orgies of the Mother in Lydia, in connection with which he was so loved by the goddess that Zeus in jealousy sent a wild boar into the fields of Lydia, which killed Atys. Both versions show that the youth held in Cybele's mysteries a position similar to that of Adonis with Aphrodite and of Osiris with Isis, [76] but it seems to have been the peculiar characteristic of the cult of Cybele that her companion was a Gallus. The fact which stands out conspicuously in all the records of the Pessinuntian rites is the service of effeminate priests, [77] who apparently represent him. In this there is probably a clue to the connection between Cretan Rhea and Phrygian Cybele, for in the two sets of cult legends there is frequent mention of the Dactyli, who belong both to Cretan and Trojan Ida. [78] Their evident association with metallurgy recalls the iron sickle produced by Gaea and given to Cronus to accomplish the overthrow of Uranus. [79]

The underlying idea in the cult of Cybele seems to have been that of an earth-goddess of fertility in man, beast, and field. Her worship was accompanied by the sound of crashing drums and cymbals, the music of the pipe, and the voices of frenzied votaries. Of her inspiration came a form of holy madness, which endowed the worshipper with a sense of mystic ecstasy and supernatural strength. The best extant description of the rites is that given by Lucretius, [80] which, although it is marred by the allegorising tendency of the poet's thought, conveys an excellent impression of the tumultuous festival. The most awe-inspiring detail of the ceremonies is that beneath the joy of the throng's self-surrender to the deity there is a terrific undertone like that of the muttering drums. The fervour of rejoicing may in a moment become the curse of irresistible madness sent by the Mother. It is a presage of the mourning in the Atys of Catullus: [81]

Dea Magna, Dea Cybele, Dindymi Dea, Domina,
Procul a mea tuus sit furor omnis, hera, domo:
Alios age incitatos: alios age rabidos!"

Ancient notices speak of other priests of Cybele, less important than the Galli. These were the Cybebi and Metragyrtae, [82] mendicant friars, whose machinations at Rome were scorned by Juvenal. [83]

In the cult legends the Galli of history are probably represented by the Corybantes, about whom there is much confusion. At times they seem to belong only to Cybele's rites, at other times they are completely identified with the Curetes. Probably the tales of Corybantes and Curetes preserve the record of primitive armed dances of religious character, in honour of Phrygian Cybele and Cretan Rhea respectively. As the two deities are essentially the same, [84] so the hoplite attendants of the one are practically the same as those of the other. As each cult assumed local individuality, the myths concerning the Corybantes would gradually appear to be quite distinct from those about the Curetes. Naturally, only an initiate in the mysteries attached to either cult would possess accurate information on details, and his lips would be inevitably sealed on all important points, so that posterity must be content to remain puzzled by remarks like this of Pausanias: [85] "In lineage the Corybantes are different from the Curetes, but, although I know the truth about both, I pass it over." Unfortunately certain writings by Epimenides [86] which might have proved highly satisfactory to modern inquiry have perished. In the actual ceremonies performed at Cybele's shrines the original warlike character [87] was almost lost in the mystic frenzy which found expression in noisy shouting and self-affliction, but it is doubtless to be traced in the measured beating of drums, the clashing of cymbals, and the music of the pipe, which set the rhythm for the ecstatic motions of the worshippers. It was expressed also in the political and warlike aspect of the goddess thus adored.[88] The Cretan legends told that the Phrygian Corybantes were summoned to the island, where by beating their shields with their swords they drowned the cries of the new-born Zeus from the ears of his jealous father, and so originated the Pyrrhic dance in which the later Curetes honoured Rhea, by moving to and fro in measured time, nodding their crested helmets, and striking their shields.[89]

The Curetes are, moreover, confounded with the Dactyli, who are usually given as five in number,--Heracles, Paeonius, Epimedes, Jasion, and Idas,[90] --the metallurgists of Cretan and Trojan Ida, also with the mysterious Ἄνακτες παῖδες, who are either the Dioscuri or the Cabiri.[91] Idas is the name, not only of a Curete, but likewise of one of the Messenian rivals and counterparts of the Spartan Διόσκουροι;[92] Jasion is the name of the mortal whom Demeter loved in Crete,[93] and who with her belongs to the mysteries of Samothrace; the Dactyl Heracles, whom Pausanias[94] carefully distinguishes from Alcmena's son, is by this writer[95] very cleverly identified with the deity of this name worshipped at Erythrae in Ionia, at Tyre, and even at Mycalessus in Boeotia. The Cabiri, being confounded with the Dactyli, are brought into close relation to the Curetes. On the other hand, they are confused with the Corybantes through Corybas, son of Jasion and Demeter, who was said to have introduced his mother's worship into Phrygia from Samoth-race.[96]

Of the Cabiric mysteries very little can be said with certainty, except that Demeter was here revered as the mother of Plutus by Jasion. Herodotus,[97] himself an initiate, believes the mysteries of Samothrace to be of Pelasgic origin. He hints at a connection between these rites and the Pelasgians' introducing herms at Athens. Furthermore, he describes [98] the type under which the Cabiri were portrayed in plastic art, that of a pygmy man, precisely like the pataïci, or grotesque figure-heads which the Phoenician triremes carried. Excavations at the Cabirium in Thebes have yielded a unique class of vases which confirm his statement. [99] Their chief interest, apart from the peculiarities of technique, is in the frank caricature shown in the painted figures. The scenes are chiefly Dionysiac in character, from which it is to be inferred that the Theban Cabirus was a form of Dionysus, but this hardly agrees with the words of Pausanias, [100] who uses the plural number of the Cabiri at Thebes. He says that he is not at liberty to reveal anything about them, nor about the acts which were performed there in honour of the Mother, that he can only say that there was once a city on this spot, that there were certain men called Cabiri, among whom were Prometheus and his son, Aetnaeus, and that the mysteries were given by Demeter to the Cabiri. This account favours Welcker's theory [101] that the Cabiri were the "Burners." In this capacity they would approach closely to the Dactyli. But they are not for this reason necessarily divorced from companionship with Dionysus, whom Pindar [102] calls the paredros of Demeter: Χαλκοκρότου πάρεδρον Δημήτερος. The epithet Χαλκοκρότου shows the intimate bond between Demeter and the Mother of the Gods. [103] Dionysus is placed naturally at the side of the former, since his worship, in cult and in legend, is to be classed with that of the Great Mother of Phrygia, Rhea's double. [104] Demeter is indeed, the Earth-Mother of Greece, on whose cult ideas were grafted which belonged to the ceremonial of the Mother in Phrygia and Lydia. [105]

So it is not strange that the Samothracian goddess closely approximates the form of Cybele, and that we find the Amazons consecrating this island to the Mother of the Gods.[106] But there is room for much conjecture concerning the meaning of the connection between the Amazons and the deity of Samothrace.[107] It is probable that there is some bearing on this in the legend of the settlement of Samothrace recorded by Pausanias.[108] This tells that the people of Samos, driven out by Androclus and the Ephesians, fled to this island, and named it Samothrace in place of the older name, Dardania. The charge which Androclus had brought against the Samian exiles was that they had joined the Carians in plotting against the Ionians. It would appear then that these colonists of Samothrace were bound by strong ties, probably of blood, to the pre-Ionic population of Ephesus and its environs, by whom the shrine of Ephesian Artemis was founded, a shrine indissolubly connected with the Amazon tradition.[109] With these facts must be considered the opinion of Herodotus that the Samothracian mysteries were of Pelasgian origin.

In Samothrace there were also Corybantic rites of Hecate.

These were performed in the Zerynthian cave,[110] from which Apollo and Artemis derived an epithet.[111] The sacrifice of dogs to Hecate held a prominent place in these mysteries. This sacrificial rite is so infrequent in Greek religion that it commands special attention wherever it is found. The Corybantic rites of Samothrace show that Hecate of this place was closely akin to the goddess of the same name, who was worshipped with Zeus Panamerius at Lagina in Caria, the chief centre of her cult in Asia Minor.[112] Strabo[113] classes her cult as Phrygian-Thracian. Farnell[114] comments on the close connection between Artemis Pheraea of Thessaly and this Hecate and suggests Thrace as the home of the cult. Some supporting evidence for this opinion may be obtained by comparing with the statement that dogs were offered to Hecate in Samothrace a remark of Sextus Empiricus,[115] that the Thracians used this animal for food.

In Lemnos there were similar Corybantic rites in honour of Bendis, who is thus brought into relationship with Samothracian Cybele and her reflex Hecate, as well as with Cretan Rhea.[116] This "Great Goddess" of Lemnos is Thracian Bendis, the fierce huntress of the two spears and the double worship, "of the heavens and of the earth," who received human sacrifice in her own country.[117] She entered the Greek pantheon as Thracian Artemis, closely allied to Cybele and Hecate. She has a counterpart in Φωσφόρος, from whom the Thracian Bosphorus was named, a goddess in whose rites the torch has a conspicuous place.[118]

Thus a long list may be made out of female deities who show the general characteristics of Phrygian Cybele: the Lydian Mother, Cybebe or Cybele; Rhea of Crete; Hecate of Samothrace and Lagina; Bendis of Thrace and Lemnos; Cappadocian Mâ;[119] Britomartis, or Dictynna, of Crete, who is Aphaea at Aegina;[120] the Syrian goddess of Hierapolis;[121] several forms of Artemis,--of the Tauric Chersonese, of Brauron, of Laodicea[122] of Ephesus,[123] Artemis-Aphrodite of Persia.[124] The conception common to all these is that of a nature-goddess, whose rites are orgiastic, and whose protection, as that of a woman-warrior, is claimed for the state. It is probably correct to assume that Artemis Tauropolos, to whom Diodorus[125] says that the Amazons offered sacrifice, is a form of Cybele, presumably Tauric Artemis. Therefore this name should be added to the list. It deserves special prominence, because the Amazons are shown to have been her votaries. In connection with Aphrodite, who, like Artemis, although less frequently, was identified with the Mother, Arnobius[126] relates that in a frenzy of devotion to this deity the daughter of a Gallus cut off her breasts, a story strikingly reminiscent of the tradition of single-breasted Amazons, and also suggestive of the fact that there were Galli in certain forms of Aphrodite's worship. [127]

The cult of Cybele seems to have been an indigenous religion in Phrygia and Lydia, [128] duplicated in almost all its essential details by that of Cretan Rhea. Since the Cretan rites of the Mother, in all probability, belonged originally to the Eteocretan population of the island, a non-Hellenic folk apparently, who seem to have been akin to the Asiatic folk not far away, [129] Rhea-Cybele may fairly be regarded as the deity of a common stock in Crete, Phrygia, and Lydia. From the circumstance that the double-axe is a religious symbol which occurs frequently wherever there are remains of the pre-Hellenic, or "Minoan," civilisation of Crete and of that thence derived, the "Mycenaean," and from the fact that in historic times this appears as the regular symbol of various forms of the Asiatic Mother, [130] there is ground for the inference that the stock with whom the worship of Rhea-Cybele was deeply rooted was that which predominated in Crete and the other lands where the same brilliant culture flourished before the rise of the Hellenic states. It is to be noted that the battle-axe of the Amazons is this very weapon, but the point may not be pressed in this context. Herodotus, [131] it has been seen, asserted out of his knowledge as an initiate, that the mysteries of Samothrace were of Pelasgic origin. He undoubtedly conceived of the Pelasgians as a non-Hellenic race who preceded the Hellenes in the occupation of Greece, and therefore we must interpret his remarks about the Cabiria as meaning that these rites were instituted by a pre-Hellenic people. [132] It is tempting to identify this people with the pre-Ionic inhabitants of Samos, who, according to Pausanias, [133] settled Samothrace. Thus the worshippers of Cybele in Samothrace would be shown to be akin to the stock who honoured her in Crete, [134] Lydia, and Phrygia.

This Mother, whose worship was widely spread under her own name and many others, was revered by the Amazons in the primitive baetylic form of the rites of Pessinus; as Mother of the Gods in Samothrace, where she was identified both with Cabiric Demeter and with Hecate; as Artemis Tauropolos, or the Tauric Virgin, who was probably a goddess of the Thracians. [135]

EPHESIAN ARTEMIS

THE magnificent temple of which Christian writers speak as that of "the great goddess whom all Asia and the world worshippeth" replaced the earlier and more famous shrine which burned to the ground on the night of Alexander's birth. Two hundred and twenty years had been spent in the process of building the first temple, and when this was destroyed the Ephesians at once began the construction of another even more costly. [136] The older Artemisium is said to have possessed among its treasures four statues of Amazons executed by four of the most distinguished sculptors of the fifth century, Phidias, Polyclitus, Cresilas, and Phradmon. [137] The tradition is only one of many which indicate very close connection between the Amazons and this sanctuary.

The Ephesians themselves looked upon their Artemisium as one of the most sacred spots in the whole world. Tacitus [138] remarks: "Primi omnium Ephesii adiere, memorantes non, ut vulgus crederat, Dianam atque Apollinem Delo genitos: esse apud se Cenechrium amnem, lucum Ortygiam, ubi Latonam partu gravidam et oleae, quae tum etiam maneat, adnisam, edidisse ea numina." This seems to mean that the olive of Ephesian Artemis was set up against the palm of Delian Apollo. Something of this kind happened historically, as Thucydides [139] shows: "There was of old a great gathering of the Ionians at Delos. . . . They went thither to the theoric assembly with their wives and children, just as the Ionians now gather at the Ephesia."

Greek Ephesus owed its origin to the Ionic Immigration and was reckoned among the twelve cities of Ionia, yet in the band of colonists who started out from the Prytaneum at Athens the Ionians were few, although the expedition is designated by their name. Joined with them were the Abantes of Euboea, the Orchomenian Minyae and the Cadmeans of Boeotia, the Dryopes, Phocians, Molossians, the Arcadian Pelasgians, the Dorian Epidaurians, and other tribes whom Herodotus does not mention by name. [140] It may be that the Ionian strain was less strong at Ephesus than in some of the other cities of the group, since this place and Colophon were the only ones of the twelve that did not take part at the Apaturia, the great clan festival of the Ionians. [141] Yet the Codrids, who figured prominently as conductors of the undertaking, were Ionians, [142] and Androclus, son of Codrus himself, was by some [143] believed to have been the founder of Ephesus. Pausanias was told that he fell in battle against the Carians and was shown his tomb at Ephesus. [144]

Pausanias [145] represents Androclus, whom he calls "king of the Ionians who sailed to Ephesus," the founder of the Ionic city, but he believes the shrine of Artemis there to be very ancient. He states with certainty that it antedated the Ionic Immigration by many years, being older even than the oracular shrine of Apollo at Didymi. He attributes its establishment to autochthons, Coresus, [146] who was son of Caÿster, and Ephesus. He says that the pre-Ionic inhabitants of the city were Leleges and Lydians--with a predominance of the latter--and that, although Androclus drove out of the land all those whom he found in the upper city, he did not interfere with those who dwelt about the sanctuary. By giving and receiving pledges he put these on a footing of neutrality. These remarks of Pausanias find confirmation in the form of the cult in historic times, which, being in all its essentials non-Hellenic, admits of plausible interpretation only as an indigenous worship taken over by the Greek settlers.

The Artemisium at Ephesus was pre-eminently a shrine which gave rights of sanctuary to suppliants, a fact indicative of a wide difference between this goddess and the Greek Artemis.[147] Those who invoked the protection of the sanctuary appeared with olive-boughs twined with fillets of wool.[148]

The Amazons are noticed in legend as founders of the shrine and as fugitives claiming its asylum. Pindar[149] told that they established the sanctuary on their way to Athens to war against Theseus. Possibly this is the account followed by Callimachus[150] in the lines telling how the Amazons set up the βρέτας of Artemis "in the shade of an oak with goodly trunk[151] which grew in Ephesus by the sea." Justin[152] states the tradition that the city itself was founded by the Amazons. Pausanias[153] maintains that Pindar was incorrect in his assertion that the shrine was founded by the Amazons. He says that long before they started on their Attic campaign they had twice taken refuge at the Artemisium, once from Heracles, and, earlier still, from Dionysus. Tacitus,[154] continuing his quotation of claims put forward by the Ephesians themselves, says: "Mox Liberum patrem, bello victorem, supplicibus Amazonum, quae aram insederant, ignovisse. Auctam hinc concessu Herculis, cum Lydia poteretur, caerimoniam templo." According to this the Amazons inaugurated the custom of seeking asylum at the Artemisium, and to them therefore was due the conspicuous part which the shrine played as a place of sanctuary. It is reasonable to infer from these various sources that in the holy records and traditions of the Ephesian temple the Amazons were prominent. Even Pausanias, who denies that the Amazons founded the shrine, ascribes to their fame, since they were reported its founders, a large measure of the prestige which belonged to the cult of Ephesian Artemis all over the Greek world. He mentions this first in his list of reasons for the great reputation of the shrine, placing it on a par with the extreme antiquity of the sanctuary. Secondary to these two he mentions the wealth and influence of the city and the epiphany of the goddess there. [155] We must, indeed, believe that the Amazons stood in intimate relation to the cult of Ephesian Artemis. Yet in historical times there was a regulation which forbade women to enter the sanctuary. [156]

Apart from her name it would be difficult to recognise the Greek Artemis in the deity of Ephesus. The cult statue showed her in form at once primitive and Oriental. [157] It was carved out of a block of wood, [158] shaped like a herm in the lower part, showing the feet. The torso was that of a woman of many breasts. The type depicted on coins [159] is that of a draped woman of many breasts, wearing a turret-crown on her head and resting either arm on a twisted column. She was served by eunuch priests, called Megabyzi, and by maidens. Presumably these priests are the same as the Essenes, whom Pausanias mentions as servitors for one year, who were bound by strict rules of chastity and required to submit to ascetic regulations of dietary and ablution. [160] The virgins associated with them passed through three stages: Postulant, Priestess, Past-Priestess. [161] There is nothing to indicate the length of their term of service. The Megabyzi were held in the highest possible honour, [162] as were the Galli at Pessinus.

This goddess of the turret-crown and of many breasts, whose shrine required the attendance of the Megabyzi, is certainly a form of Cybele. If we were guided solely by the remark of Pausanias [163] that the sanctuary was founded by the pre-Ionic people of the region, that is, by Leleges and Lydians, among whom the latter were more numerous, we should expect to find the Lydian Mother worshipped here. The name Artemis, under which the goddess appears, indicates that the Greek colonists appropriated the cult which they found. The Lydian Mother was evidently identical with Magna Mater of Phrygia. Yet the Ephesian goddess, who is the Mother under the name Artemis, is in her cult image neither Cybele as we know her--whether under baetylic form or in the likeness of a matron [164]--nor Hellenic Artemis. Artemidorus, [165] the student of dreams, says that peculiar sanctity attached to a particular type which he defines as that of Artemis Ephesia, Artemis of Perge, and the goddess called Eleuthera among the Lycians. It is tempting to ascribe to the mysterious Leleges the differences which separate the type of Ephesia and the other two from Cybele.

All that Pausanias [166] tells about these Leleges at Ephesus is that they were a branch of the Carians. Herodotus [167] says that the Leleges were a people who in old times dwelt in the islands of the Aegean and were subject to Minos of Crete; that they were driven from their homes by the Dorians and Ionians, after which they took refuge in Caria and were named Carians. It seems reasonable to give weight to the remarks of Herodotus on this subject, since he was a Carian-born Ionian. We should infer then that the Leleges of Ephesus, whom Pausanias calls a branch of the Carians, were closely connected with the island-people who were once subject to Minos. Both Herodotus [168] and Pausanias [169] say that the Lycians were of Cretan origin. It is therefore not strange that at Ephesus and in Lycia the same type of goddess was worshipped. Tradition [170] also connected Pamphy-lia with Crete, which may account for the presence of the type in Perge. [171] An inscription [172] which dates probably from about the third century B.C. gives direct evidence of association between Crete and Ephesian Artemis. It is the dedication of a votive offering: "To the Healer of diseases, to Apollo, Giver of Light to mortals, Eutyches has set up in votive offering (a statue of) the Cretan Lady of Ephesus, the Light-Bearer (ἄνασσαν Ἐφέσου Κρησίαν φαεσφόρον." The inscription suggests the words from the Oedipus Rex: [173] "Lyceian Lord, scatter, I pray thee, for our aid thine unconquerable darts from thy gold-twisted bowstring and with them the fire-bearing rays of Artemis with which she rusheth over the Lycian mountains." The Cretan Light-Bearer may easily be the fire-bearing Artemis of Lycia. The epithet Λύκειος used of Apollo gives the form Λυκεία for Artemis. An Artemis by this name was worshipped at Troezen. [174] The local exegetes were unable to explain the application of the epithet. Therefore Pausanias conjectures that it means, either that Hippolytus had thus commemorated the extermination of wolves at Troezen, or that Λυκεία was a cult epithet among the Amazons, to whom Hippolytus was akin through his mother. It seems highly probable that Artemis Λυκεία was the goddess of Ephesus, Perge, and Lycia, who was known as the Cretan Lady of Ephesus.

Eleuthera, the special name by which this Artemis was worshipped among the Lycians suggests Ariadne, whom Ovid [175] calls Libera. [176] The name belongs to her as the wife of Dionysus in Crete. Dionysus appears in the legends of the Artemisium as one of the foes of the Amazons who drove them to this asylum. [177] Perhaps the idea of hostility on his part is to be explained by the rites in his honour at the annual festival of the Scierea at Alea. These required that women should be scourged at his altar. [178] In this there is reminiscence of the Egyptian mournings for Osiris, which were marked with practices of self-affliction, and Osiris suggests Atys, the companion of the Asiatic Mother. [179] There is no reason to doubt that Dionysus was closely connected with Cybele. The musical system by which his worship was characterised was Phrygian, [180] and Euripides in the Bacchae completely identifies his rites with those of the Mother. We hear also of men who marched in procession at his festivals with cymbals and tambourines. [181] Considering the fact that at Ephesus and at Pessinus there were eunuch priests, also that Euripides [182] depicts Dionysus as a womanish person who forces Pentheus to assume woman's garments, that elsewhere [183] the god is called man and woman, and, in addition to this, that there was a legend [184] that he received woman's attire from Rhea at Cybela, there is a strong presumption in favour of the hypothesis that Dionysus touches the cult of the Great Mother and that of Ephesian Artemis in some way associated with the strange Oriental idea of confusion of sex. [185] If this interpretation is correct, it probably applies also to the rites of Ariadne, for at Athens in the feast of the Oschophoria two youths dressed as women conducted a chorus in honour of Dionysus and Ariadne. [186]

The Ephesian legend of Heracles and the Amazons [187] probably indicates a connection between the cult of Ephesian Artemis and that of the Lydian Heracles. This cult of Heracles is reflected in Greek legend as the adventure of the hero at the court of Omphale. The story runs thus: [188] Heracles was compelled to submit to slavery to this Lydian queen in order that he might recover from the madness which punished him for his murder of Eurytus. Omphale, who was daughter of Dardanus and widow of Tmolus, became enamoured of her captive and married him. He gave up to her his weapons and received in return woman's dress and the distaff. He is represented sitting among the maidens and allowing the queen to beat him with her sandals whenever he has erred in spinning. The names Dardanus and Tmolus suggest, the former, Mount Ida and Samothrace, the latter, Lydia. It is noteworthy that Pausanias [189] identifies this Oriental Heracles with the Idaean Dactyl of that name. Omphale is presumably Magna Mater, and probably the detail of the gift of the weapons [190] to her points to the fact that this goddess was warlike and political in Asia Minor. In this legend, as also in that which connects the Amazons with Dionysus, there appears the peculiar Asiatic idea of sex-confusion. [191] Granted a close connection between the Oriental Heracles and the Amazons at Ephesus, [192] the supposition does not seem audacious that the most widely spread of all the Hellenic traditions concerning the

Amazons, that of the attack by Heracles on Themiscyra, owed its origin to a cult saga typified by that of Ephesus.

To summarise: There was close connection between the Amazons and Ephesian Artemis, a type of the Mother showing Cretan-Lycian affiliations. Their place in the cult gave rise to the two local sagas which emphasise the Oriental idea of sex-confusion.

ARTEMIS ASTRATEIA AND APOLLO AMAZONIUS

PAUSANIAS [193] says that there were two ways of accounting for the name of the town Pyrrhichus in southern Greece. One derived it from Pyrrhus, son of Achilles, the other, from Pyrrhichus, a god of "the so-called Curetes." There was also a local story that the town was settled by Silenus from Malea. Pausanias adds that the people about Malea explained how Silenus came to be called Pyrrhichus also, but he does not give the explanation. He concludes his remarks about the town with these words: "In the market-place there is a well of water which they believe was given to them by Silenus. There would be a dearth of water, if this well should fail. The gods who have sanctuaries in their land are Artemis, surnamed Astrateia, because the Amazons here ceased their forward march, and Apollo Amazonius. The statues are both xoana, and they say that they were set up by the women from the Thermodon."

Thus the sole mention of these two cult-epithets, presumably of great value to the investigator of the Amazon tradition, occurs in a passage which offers no help toward understanding them and in a puzzling context. It is strange to hear of the Amazons in Laconia, a canton in no way associated with the stock tale, as we know it, of the invasion of Attica. The few words in Pausanias suggest that the legend at Pyrrhichus told of the halting of a large army. In this it would differ from the Boeotian tradition [194] of a small band of Amazons separated from the rest in their rout by Theseus. There is no mention of a goal, whether Athens or Troezen, toward which the army that halted in Laconia were directing their campaign.

It seems natural to name Apollo and Artemis together, yet the Artemis of Ephesus, with whom the Amazons were closely associated, and Artemis Tauropolos, also mentioned as a goddess whom they worshipped, are in no way like the companion of the Hellenic Apollo. The obvious course of reasoning is to assume that Astrateia is the Asiatic Artemis and that, therefore, Apollo Amazonius is fundamentally a non-Hellenic god.

Although Apollo is pre-eminently a Greek divinity, the same name was used of a god worshipped in the Troad before the times of the earliest Aeolic colonisation. The only attributes of this deity, whose epithet was Smintheus, were the bow and the gift of prophecy.[195] Throughout the Iliad Apollo appears as a Trojan rather than a Greek ally, a fact not without significance to this inquiry. Cicero[196] mentions three gods called Apollo: the son of Hephaestus and Athena, the son of Corybas, and the son of Zeus and Leto. Of the second, who would seem to belong to cults related to that of the Mother, it was said that he was born in Crete, and that he contended with Zeus himself for the possession of the island. He is elsewhere called a son of Corybas, but this is the only reference to his struggle with Zeus.[197] This Apollo might appropriately be paired with an Artemis of the type of Ephesia. The sole hint at a ritual relation between Artemis and Apollo at Ephesus is in the inscription quoted above,[198] which records the dedication of a statue of "the Cretan Lady of Ephesus, the Light-Bearer" to Apollo, "Healer of diseases and Giver of Light to mortals." It was found to be not improbable that the Cretan Lady was the goddess whom the Lycians worshipped under the type of Ephesia, and to whom as Λυκεία Hippolytus dedicated a temple at Troezen. Sophocles[199] emphasises the bow as the attribute of Apollo Λύκειος, the companion of Artemis of Lycia. With this should be considered the fact that Apollo had three oracular shrines in Asia Minor,--at Branchidae, Clarus, and Patara in Lycia. Then the gift of prophecy as well as the bow, the two attributes of Apollo Smintheus may both be assigned to the Lycian Apollo. The hypothesis may be stated: that the Phrygian-Lycian Apollo, closely allied to Artemis Λυκεία, the Lycian type of Ephesia, is Apollo Amazonius. The theory tends to reconcile two conflicting statements, the one that of Pindar,[200] who represents Apollo as friendly to the Amazons, the other that of Macrobius,[201] who tells that he assisted Theseus and Heracles against them. Apollo, conceived as the Hellenic god, would naturally be their enemy, while the Asiatic Apollo would be their patron. It is possible to explain in the same way the seeming inconsistency shown in representing the defeat of the Amazons on the walls of the temple at Bassae.

It has been assumed in the preceding paragraph that Artemis Astrateia, because she is a goddess of the Amazons, is practically identical with Ephesia, and on this assumption an hypothetical interpretation of Apollo Amazonius has been based. In order that the investigation may be pursued from a different point of view, this argument may be dismissed for the present, to give place to an inquiry concerning the meaning of Astrateia. Farnell[202] does not discuss the epithet Amazonius, but for Astrateia he proposes the explanation that the word is a linguistic corruption for Astarte. By this theory the connection with a στρατεία denotes only a local attempt to account for a word of which the real significance was completely lost. The position of Pyrrhichus on the Laconian coast makes it easily credible that foreign influences might have imported the Semitic goddess. As the theory is put forward tentatively, details are not elaborated, and so it is not stated whether there is any reason other than caprice for connecting the Amazons, rather than another army, with the imaginary στρατεία. Rouse[203] accepts the statement of Pausanias as it stands and renders the phrase "Artemis of the War-host."

If Astrateia be "Artemis of the War-host," she was presumably an armed goddess. Pausanias [204] records that there was a statue of Artemis in Messenia bearing shield and spear. At Laodicea there was the conception of an armed Artemis, as shown by coins, and since the Laodiceans claimed to possess the original cult statue of the Brauronian goddess, [205] who was identified with the Tauric Virgin, [206] there is reason to believe that these two types of Artemis, Brauronia and Taurica, depicted her as an armed goddess. Furthermore, Artemis appears as a goddess of battle in her cult as Agrotera, for she regularly received sacrifice from the Spartans before a campaign or a battle; [207] at Athens the polemarch, assisted by the ephebes, in commemoration of Marathon sacrificed annually to her in conjunction with Enyalius; [208] and at Aegaera in Achaea she was believed to have routed the Sicyonians by telling the people of Aegaera to bind torches to the horns of a flock of goats in order to terrify the enemy. [209] Artemis Laphria, a Calydonian deity, is possibly also a goddess of war. She is pre-eminently a huntress, and in this respect might resemble Thracian Bendis, who entered the Greek pantheon as Artemis. Pausanias [210] seems to hint that the type of Laphria is related to that of Ephesia. Ephesia and Bendis both are forms of the Mother, who in Asia was warlike. [211]

But not one of these epithets of warlike Artemis is suggestive of the word Astrateia. The nearest approach to it is in three surnames of Aphrodite,--Strateia at Mylasa, [212] Strategis at Paros, [213] and Stratonikis at Smyrna, [214] of which the first is startlingly similar to the one under consideration. The only epithet among those used of Artemis which calls Astrateia is Hegemone.

Artemis Hegemone was worshipped at Tegea, at Sparta, and near Acacesium in Arcadia. About her cult at Tegea there is nothing told which would differentiate this from other types.[215] At Sparta she was worshipped with Eileithyia and Apollo Carneüs in a shrine near the Dromos.[216] Eileithyia seems to have been a primitive goddess, whose worship was pre-Hellenic, and who in classical Greek times was identified with Artemis as helper of women in travail.[217] The torch was prominent in her ritual. Apollo Carneüs is generally known as the patron of the Dorian race. There are frequent notices of him in ancient literature as the god of the conquering people of Lacedaemon, a warrior who, like Mars at Rome, presides also over the flocks and herds.[218] Yet Pausanias[219] tells a story which makes it highly probable that among the pre-Dorian folk of Sparta there was a god of prophecy whose worship was grafted on that of Hellenic Apollo, whence there was formed the type of Carneüs. Pausanias distinguishes between a man named Carneüs and Apollo Carneüs. The former, who was surnamed Οἰκέτας, lived in pre-Dorian Sparta, and was highly honoured in the family of a prophet named Crius. In Dorian times there was a prophet of an Acarnanian family who was killed at Sparta by Hippotes. Apollo therefore was wrathful, and the Dorians exiled the criminal and atoned for the murder. The cult name of Apollo Carneüs was formed from the name of this Acarnanian prophet. It will be observed that in both legends there is mention of prophecy, a fact strongly suggestive of the Phrygian Apollo. Pausanias in this context relates a third story which brings Apollo Carneüs into direct connection with Troy. He tells that when the Greeks were making the wooden horse, they used wood of a cornel-tree (κράνεια) cut in the sacred grove of Apollo. As soon as they learned that the god was angry at their presumption they propitiated him under the name Carneüs. It seems not unreasonable to infer from these three legends that, although Apollo Carneüs came to be regarded as the Dorians' god, he was in a measure identical with the prophet-god of Phrygia and Lycia. The inference is strengthened by a fourth account in the same context. In this Pausanias quotes Praxilla, who said that Carneüs was from Crete, since he was the son of Europa and Zeus, foster-child of Apollo and Leto. In further support of the theory, here stated tentatively, it should be added that Acarnania, the home of the prophet who was killed at Sparta by the Dorians, was the country of the Curetes, conceived as one of the pre-Hellenic races of Greece.[220] Their name points to Crete. It must also be said that many believed Eileithyia to be of Cretan origin.[221] Thus Eileithyia, the third in the group worshipped at Sparta, may have been connected with the cult of the Apollo of Phrygia, Lycia, and Crete. In the shrine of Artemis Hegemone near Acacesium the cult statue showed the goddess with torches in her hands.[222] This temple gave access to the sanctuary of Despoena[223] in which Demeter was worshipped as the mother of Despoena. The cult legend made Artemis the child of Demeter rather than of Leto. Therefore beside the throne of Demeter there was a statue of Artemis, who was represented as a huntress with quiver, hunting dog, and a mantle of stag's skin. In one hand she carried a torch, in the other two serpents. Since the temple of Artemis Hegemone gave access to this shrine, and since in the attribute of the torch the statue in the inner sanctuary resembled that in the outer temple, it seems probable that the Artemis of the Despoena temple was Artemis Hegemone. In this sanctuary the Great Mother was worshipped with Demeter and Despoena, and the initiates heard holy tales about the Titans,[224] Curetes, and Corybantes, all of whom were connected with Corybantes, all of whom were connected with orgiastic rites--the first, with those of Dionysus, the second and third, with those of Rhea-Cybele. It would follow that Artemis Hegemone belonged to the circle of deities honoured by mystic ceremonies like those of Crete and Asia Minor. Miss Harrison[225] mentions the torch as a conspicuous feature in the cult of Artemis Hegemone and connects her closely with Hecate who was Φωσφόρος; on the shores of the Thracian Bosphorus. The identification between Hecate and the Mother has already been noticed. [226]

The investigation of Hegemone as an epithet would be incomplete without the mention of the use of the word in three other instances: alone, as the name of a goddess; as surname of Aphrodite; in adjectival form Ἡγεμόνιος; as an epithet of Hermes. The first of these shows Hegemone as the name of one of the divinities by whom the Athenian ephebes swore: "Be ye judges of the oath, Agraulus, Enyalius, Ares, Zeus, Thallo, Auxo, Hegemone." [227] Agraulus, Thallo, Auxo, and Hegemone appear to have been old deities of the soil. Pausanias [228] gives Thallo as one of the two Horae whom the Athenians worshipped with Pandrosus. He gives Auxo and Hegemone as the two Charites who had been revered at Athens from of old ἐκ παλαιοῦ) [229] The evidence for the worship of Aphrodite Hegemone is an altar basis found on the Acropolis at Athens with the inscription: Ἀφροδίτῃ ἡγεμόνῃ τοῦ δήμου. [230] Epigraphical evidence also furnishes the epithet Hegemonius with Hermes. The inscription [231] comes from the site of the Metroüm at the Piraeus, where Atys was worshipped with the Mother, and it is therefore presumable that this Hermes belongs in some way to this Asiatic cult.

It is possible to interpret Hegemone as an epithet indicating warlike character. The phrase, "leader of the people," applied to Aphrodite at Athens, suggests this. The Hegemone whom the ephebes invoked may have been regarded as such a leader. That as a Charis she was a primitive goddess of the soil tends to support the theory, inasmuch as early divinities are frequently both givers of fertility and protectors of their people in battle. It has been seen that this was the case with Apollo Carneüs at

Sparta. It is noteworthy that there he was associated with Artemis Hegemone. This combination of qualities is displayed by the Great Mother and those resembling her. It has been noted that the Arcadian cult of Artemis Hegemone was in some way closely related to that of Despoena, a goddess whose rites were connected with the Corybantic rites of Demeter and the Asiatic Mother. Furthermore, the likeness between Artemis Hegemone and Hecate confirms the theory.

But whether Artemis Hegemone gained her epithet from a warlike character or not, she is undeniably a goddess whose attribute was the torch, and in this she approaches several of those forms of Artemis which are admitted to be martial. [232] Artemis Agrotera was a huntress like the Artemis, probably Hegemone, beside the throne of Demeter in the sanctuary of Despoena. Like her, and also like the Artemis of the outer shrine, who was certainly Artemis Hegemone, she was a goddess of the torch. The fact comes out in the story of the rout of the Sicyonian army at Aegaera. In the version which the Pseudo-Plutarch gives of the ceremony in which the Polemarch and ephebes sacrificed at Athens in memory of Marathon he substitutes Hecate for Artemis Agrotera, the name given by Pollux. Artemis Laphria, who seems to have resembled Ephesia, was honoured at Patrae in Achaea in an annual festival of fire. [233] Into an enclosure about her altar all sorts of wild beasts were driven to be burned alive. Like Agrotera, and, presumably, like Hegemone, she was a huntress. Another huntress was Thracian Bendis, who was nearly related to Hecate and the Mother, and who was taken over by the Greeks as a form of Artemis. Her rites required torches. [234]

The torch does not appear as a feature in the Hellenic worship of Artemis until the fifth century B.C. After that its connection with the cult becomes steadily more and more prominent. Its association with this goddess may be traced historically to the influence of orgiastic rituals from Thrace and Asia Minor, like those of the Mother and Dionysus, and it is to be explained by the tendency to identify Artemis with various forms of Magna Mater.[235] The inference is inevitable that the three types of Artemis,--Agrotera, Hegemone, and Laphria--approach one which may be called Thracian-Phrygian, probably that of Hecate, in so far as she is similar to Cybele. These three forms of Artemis are warlike in character, but it is impossible to state with certainty that any one of them was represented in the cult image as an armed goddess. Such a statement can be made only of the statue of Artemis at Laodicea and of that which Pausanias saw at Messene. We possess no further record of the latter, but we are practically sure that the former was the type surnamed Taurica and Brauronia.[236] Since the home of this cult was the Tauric Chersonese, where the goddess was called the Virgin, the type must be classed as Thracian, and since it resembles that of Rhea-Cybele and Artemis Ephesia, it may properly be called Thracian-Phrygian. Thus not only the forms of Artemis which imply a warlike character, but also those which represented her armed, indicate that the cult came from the countries where the chief deity was a woman, both Mother and Warrior. It follows, that if Artemis Astrateia be Artemis "of the War-host," she is closely akin to the type of the Mother. In other words, she is, as it was at first conjectured, very like Ephesia and Tauropolos.

It remains to consider the possibility that she is Astarte. Cicero[237] remarks that Astarte of Syria was identified with Aphrodite, and that in this conception she appears as the wife of Adonis. Herein the type of Aphrodite approximates that of Cybele in Lydia and Phrygia where Atys corresponds to Adonis. At Hierapolis the Syrian goddess described by the Pseudo-Lucian has characteristics of Artemis as well as Aphrodite. In these rites the torch was a prominent feature, as in those of the Thracian-

Phrygian Mother. Thus Artemis Astarte might be precisely the same as Warlike Artemis. Moreover, even if the goddess at Pyrrhichus were an Astarte more similar to Aphrodite than to Artemis, the probabilities would be strong in favour of the theory that she was armed, for the cult epithet of Aphrodite-Astarte in Greek religion was Urania, of whom there is reason to believe that she was the armed Aphrodite.[238] So from two hypotheses, the one, that Artemis Astrateia is Warlike Artemis, the other, that she is Astarte,[239] the inference is to be drawn that the image at Pyrrhichus showed her armed.

On the assumption that the goddess was armed it is reasonable to suppose that an armed god was grouped with her. It is easy to imagine the Hellenic Apollo defending his people, inspiring them with courage, and visiting their enemies with pestilence, yet he is not a truly martial deity under any one of these conceptions. However, his worship at Sparta as Carneüs has reminiscence of a time when he was regarded as a fighting god. Comment has already been made[240] on the indications that Carneüs was a pre-Dorian divinity of prophecy whom the Hellenes identified with their Apollo. The Phrygian god to whom he was very possibly related was a warrior in so far as the bow was as fixedly his attribute as the mantic gift. Near Sparta there was the shrine of another Apollo[241] portrayed in rude and primitive fashion in the form of a colossal bronze column, to which were added the head, hands, and feet of a man. The figure wore a helmet, and in his hands he carried spear and bow. Amyclae, the village to which his sanctuary belonged, was one of the pre-Dorian cities which had held out valiantly, but had finally been devastated by the invaders.[242] Here there was preserved down to the time of Pausanias a sanctuary of Alexandra, so-called by the Amyclaeans, who was said to be Priam's daughter Cassandra.[243] At Leuctra in Laconia this Alexandra had a temple and image, and here there were xoana of Apollo Carneüs, "made after the custom of the Lacedaemonians of Sparta."[244] Cassandra is conspicuously a prophetess who belongs to Troy and to Trojan Apollo, and therefore a relation between her cult and that of Carneüs, a god who seems to have been originally identical with the prophetic Apollo of Phrygia, Lycia, and Crete,[245] is natural. Apollo Amyclaeus resembles this Cretan-Asiatic Apollo in the attribute of the bow, and the helmet and spear betray his relation to Apollo Carneüs. Moreover, since at Leuctra in Laconia there was evidently a connection between the rites of Cassandra and Apollo Carneüs, the inference may be drawn that at Amyclae she stood in ritual relation to the local god. It would follow that Apollo Amyclaeus was in some way a prophet, and thus in another detail Amyclaeus resembles the pre-Dorian Carneüs. The festival of the Hyacinthia, which belonged to the Amyclaean cult, gave temporary freedom to the slaves of the region about Sparta and was a great holiday among the humbler freemen. It seems probable therefore that the feast was derived from the religion of the submerged element of the population, i. e. from the conquered aborigines. In its mystic imagery of the processes of life and death there is the hint that it was instituted in honour of a chthonic deity of fertility.[246] The legends of Amyclae certainly told of a period when the place was influential before the Dorian Invasion, and so presumably the worship of Apollo Amyclaeus was instituted by the pre-historic, or "Mycenaean," inhabitants of Laconia, whose civilisation, revealed in the artistic remains of Vaphio and in the myth of the royal house of Menelaus, was homogeneous with that termed "Minoan." The chief points in the argument are that Apollo Amyclaeus was portrayed in non-Hellenic fashion, that he was conceived, like Carneüs, as warrior and god of fertility, and that in general characteristics he seems to have been identical with the prophet-archer worshipped in Asia and in Crete.

Thus various trains of thought converge to establish the theory that the deities whom the Amazons were said to have introduced at Pyrrhichus were a warrior woman and a warrior man. The former seems to have been akin to Cybele, the Tauric Virgin, Ephesian Artemis, and others of the general type which includes these, the latter, to the god who was worshipped by the same pre-Hellenic peoples who evolved or perpetuated the rites of the Mother. He is a male divinity of battle and fertility, who was originally of secondary importance to the female. The mantic gift which belongs to him fits in well with the clamour which accompanied the ceremonies of the Mother in historical times and with the sense of possession by divine power which seized upon her worshippers. As Aeschylus clearly shows in the character of Cassandra, the skill of prophecy is divine madness. Frenzy was prominent in all orgiastic cults.

With the thought in mind that Artemis Astrateia and Apollo Amazonius are gods of the race who lived in Laconia before the Hellenes, it is important to examine the brief account which Pausanias furnishes of Pyrrhichus. [247] The town was said to have been named either from Pyrrhus or from Pyrrhichus, the latter a god of the so-called Curetes. It is natural that the epic tales about the house of Menelaus at Sparta should have been in vogue elsewhere in Laconia. Therefore the story of the coming of Pyrrhus to wed Hermione was associated with Pyrrhichus and also with Scyra [248] on a river not far away. Pausanias, however, puts more confidence in the other account of the name of the town.

The theory that Pyrrhichus was a god of the so-called Curetes implies that these are here conceived to be a primitive folk. The only region of Greece to which an early people of this name may be assigned with certainty is the land north of the Corinthian gulf. Apollodorus [249] states that the older name of

Aetolia, regarded as the tract extending from the Evenus to the Acheloüs, was Curetis, and Pausanias [250] tells that the Curetes were the earliest inhabitants of Acarnania. In the legend of Meleager, as it is preserved in the Iliad, [251] the Curetes are shown besieging Calydon, the Aetolians' city. The dispute had arisen over the division of the spoils of the famous boar-hunt. The death of Meleager, who gives his life for the city, is ascribed in the Homeric version to the prayers of his mother Althaea, who had cried on Hades and Persephone to destroy him in vengeance for his having slain her brother, a prince of the Curetes. Pausanias [252] quotes the Eoeae of Hesiod and the Minyad as authorities for the statement that he was killed by Apollo, the patron of the Curetes against the Aetolians. In the Homeric story there is a hint that Apollo was unfriendly to the Calydonians. This is in the reference to the presumption of Idas, who attempted to shoot Apollo who had ravished his wife Marpessa. By Idas she was mother of Cleopatra, the wife of Meleager. Heroic legend shows many connections between this region of Acarnania and Aetolia and that of Messenia and Laconia. At the Calydonian chase, in which the Curetes and Aetolians were allies, Idas and Lynceus of Messenia and their Laconian cousins and rivals, Castor and Polydeuces, were among the assembled chiefs who took part. [253] Idas was connected with the house of Calydon by marriage with Marpessa. [254] Thestius, brother to Marpessa's father and king of Pleuron, the city of the Curetes, married his daughter Althaea to Oeneus of Calydon [255] and his daughter Leda to Tyndareus of Sparta. [256] Thus the Dioscuri, Leda's children, were related to the Curetes of northern Greece. These genealogies originated doubtless in racial affinities between the pre-Dorians of Laconia and Messenia and the early folk of Acarnania and Aetolia. In pre-historic times Messenia and Laconia seem to have been one country, founded by Lelex, locally known as an autochthon, and its name was Lelegia. [257] The Dioscuri were worshipped from of old both in Messenia and in Laconia as θεοὶ μεγάλοι, and as such they were easily confused with the Cabiri and also with the Idaean Dactyli.[258] Thus the argument leads to a connection between this folk called Curetes and the people among whom the orgiastic worship of the Mother was indigenous, and so it seems natural that the armed dancers who attended Cretan Rhea should have been named Curetes. The mention of the Leleges in Laconia and Messenia establishes direct connections with the pre-historic "Aegean" civilisation, which was tributary to the "Minoan," and also with the early races by whom the sanctuary of Ephesian Artemis was founded.[259]

There are the same implications in the statement[260] that Pyrrhichus, a god of these Curetes, was another name for Silenus. The oldest and most persistent legends in regard to Silenus connect him with the country about the Maeander in Phrygia.[261] He belongs to the rites of Dionysus, which were intimately related to those of the Mother. The Cabiric mysteries probably combined the cult of a form of the Mother with that of Dionysus, whence arose the story that Dionysus was the son of Cabirus.[262] Dioscuri, Cabiri, Anaces, Dactyli are all in a certain sense the same. Hence we may think of this Pyrrhichus as a pre-Dorian, or "Lelegian," member of the circle of deities among whom the Mother was chief. He was probably at once Cabirus, Dactyl, and armed dancer. That he was the last is implied not only by his place among the Curetes, but also by the fact that his name is that of the famous dance at Sparta.[263]

The study of the Curetes of Laconia yields evidence in accord with that gathered from other courses of reasoning adopted above. The forerunners of the Hellenes in Laconia seem to have been akin to the people of Acarnania, where Apollo was the patron of the Curetes, the original home of the prophet Carneüs. They seem also to have been related to the race who worshipped the Mother under the type of the goddess of Ephesus.

It must be concluded, therefore, that Artemis Astrateia was a form of Ephesia, and that Apollo Amazonius was the prophet-archer who was worshipped with her at Ephesus, and whose cult belonged to Phrygians, Lycians, Cretans, and the pre-Hellenic folk of Greece.

ARES

THE legend of the Amazons was not superficially rooted at Athens. This is proved by the fact that it found expression in cult practice at one of the greater festivals of the state. Before the Thesea the Athenians annually offered sacrifice to the Amazons, thus commemorating the victory of Theseus over the women. The decisive battle was said to have been fought on the day marked by the oblation of the Boedromia.[264] Plutarch [265] bases his belief in the reality of the invasion of Attica on three points: the place names, Amazonium and Horcomosium; the presence of graves of the fallen; the yearly sacrifice to the Amazons.

The general view of ancient writers [266] is that the Amazons made the Areopagus the basis of their operations, having established their camp there in a spot thenceforth called the Amazonium [267] Aeschylus [268] derives the name of the hill itself from the fact that there the Amazons offered frequent sacrifice [269] to Ares while they held it as a citadel against the Acropolis. The statement is remarkable in view of two facts which seem to show Ares as the patron of Theseus rather than of the Amazons: Plutarch, [270] quoting Clidemus, says that before entering the critical battle with the Amazons Theseus sacrificed to Phobus, son of Ares, and hereby won the day; the tradition[271] at Troezen told that Theseus commemorated his victory over the Amazons there by dedicating a temple to Ares at the entrance to the Genethlium.

It is therefore impossible to determine the exact relation in which Ares stood to the Amazons in the story of the invasion of

Greece. All that may be said is that his name belongs to the saga of Theseus and the Amazons in the two accounts, the Attic and the Troezenian. It must be added that the saga bears the marks of great age. Herein Theseus is not an intruder, as he evidently is in the tales of the storm of Themiscyra, nor is he a substitute for Heracles. The story is primarily concerned with Theseus himself, the great hero of the two states. While in the former it is connected with ritual acts, in the latter it is hallowed by association with the Genethlium, the traditional birth-place of Theseus.[272] Moreover, on the tradition of the Amazons at Troezen rests the story of Hippolytus, whose sepulchre assured the safety of the nation.[273]

The Attic traditions about Theseus were concerned chiefly with his adventures in Crete. With retrospect toward these the Athenians celebrated the festivals of the Oschophoria, the Pyanepsia, and the Thesea. Ariadne, as it has been stated,[274] was probably a Cretan goddess, with whose worship at Athens are to be connected the rites of the Oschophoria, wherein two youths disguised as maidens led the girls' chorus. The implication is that the Oriental idea of sex confusion was associated with the festival. It seems therefore that the ceremonies instituted by Theseus reflect the Anatolian worship of Cybele. It accords with the customary restraint of Hellenic habits that the Oriental idea shown in the cults of Cybele, Ephesian Artemis, and the Syrian Goddess, manifested itself at Athens merely in a pleasing masque. The name of Theseus also connected Troezen with Crete. Phaedra, the wife with whom he lived at Troezen, is famous as the destroyer of the Amazon's son, Hippolytus, and as another princess of the house of Minos. Thus in its twofold aspect the tradition of Theseus suggests the time when "Minoan" Crete was pre-eminent. It maybe that the association of the Amazon legend with the tale of Theseus is to be ascribed to some such source. In that case Ares, a deity whose cult had slight prominence in Greece, might by reason of his place in the saga of Theseus and the Amazons, be connected with the cult of Aphrodite-Ariadne. There is this suggestion in a note from Olen which Pausanias [275] inserts in the account of his visit to the shrine of Hebe at Phlius. Olen connects Ares with Hebe as her own brother, born of Hera. Her shrine at Phlius is shown to be very old by the fact that her worship here was in the strictest sense aniconic. Her annual festival of the "Ivy-Cuttings" has al hint of Dionysus and even of the ivy-shaped shields of the Amazons. From other sources it may be gathered that she was akin to Aphrodite-Ariadne. [276]Pausanias says that Hebe was substituted for her more ancient name, Ganymeda. In this there is reminiscence of the Trojan youth caught tip to heaven by Zeus. The feminine form implies the appropriation by one sex of the characteristics of the other. This might belong naturally to a Phrygian legend.

A search for parallels to the association which Aeschylus mentions between Ares and the Amazons discovers first of all, as most striking, the legend told of the statue of Ares Γυναικο-θοίνας in the market-place at Tegea. [277]The statue was explained as the dedication of a band of Tegeate women who had won a victory over the Spartans in the time of King Charillus of Sparta. After peace was established the women instituted a festival in honour of Ares. Since men were excluded from the sacrifice and sacred banquet, the god was called "Entertainer of Women." It is interesting to find such a tale in Arcadian Tegea, the home of Atalanta, herself similar to the Amazons. It is worth bearing in mind that Atalanta won the spoils of the Calydonian hunt in the country of the Aetolians and Curetes, the kindred of the folk of pre-historic Pyrrhichus. In the temple of Athena Alea at Tegea, which contained these spoils, [278]Marpessa, leader of the women who honoured Ares, dedicated her shield. [279]

In the immediate neighbourhood of Tegea there was a shrine of Ares Ἀφνειός, [280] situated on a mountain of which the name Cresium implies the worship of Cretan Dionysus. [281] The epithet was explained by the story that Ares enabled his child Aëropus to draw milk from the breasts of his mother after her death. The mother Aërope, grand-daughter of Aleus, was akin to Atalanta. The lifetime of her child by Ares was placed in the generation preceding the Dorian Invasion. [282]

Elsewhere in Arcadia,--at Megalopolis [283] and near Acacesium [284]--there were monuments attesting the foundation of the cult of Ares in this canton in early days. With this should be compared the statement of Arnobius, [285] that there was a legend of thirteen months' servitude exacted of Ares in Arcadia. The general tendency of all the evidence is in support of the theory that the cult of Ares Γυναικοθοίνας originated in primitive times.

There were two other legends of armed women in Greece, both localised, like the Tegeate story, in the Peloponnese. A statue of Ares at Argos was explained as the dedication of a band of women under the poetess Telesilla who had won a victory over the Spartans. [286] The other legend belonged to Sparta. Here a troop of women commemorated their victory over the Messenians by founding a temple to Aphrodite. [287] The most obvious interpretation of the epithet is to derive it from Ares and to render it "Warlike." It is used of Athena in three oaths of alliance suggestive of the martial character of the goddess. [288] The Athenians built a temple to Athena Ἀρεία at Plataea, constructed from the spoils of Marathon. [289] After his acquittal on the Areopagus Orestes is said to have dedicated an altar to Athena Ἀρεία. [290] In this the reference is evidently to the name of the hill on which the court sat which the Greeks themselves, however mistaken they may have been in their etymology, certainly connected with Ares. [291]These instances of the use of the epithet favour the idea that it was derived from the name of Ares. It may be argued that Aphrodite Ἀρεία was a type of the goddess conceived as guardian of the state. In this aspect she was more frequently worshipped at Sparta than elsewhere in Greece. The probabilities are that she was represented armed.[292] This political goddess of Sparta was the Oriental Aphrodite, called Urania. The fact that one group of armed women gave special honour to Ares, another to Aphrodite Ἀρεία, is of importance to the investigation. The hint that the two deities were in some way associated suggests connection between Ares and the Anatolian cult of the warlike Mother whom the Amazons worshipped.

It would seem that the connection between Ares and the Warlike Aphrodite was not slight. At Thebes the joint cult of the two as a conjugal pair was established at an early date,[293] and their union was said to have given rise to the Cadmean family and thence to Dionysus. Through marriage with Harmonia, daughter of Ares and Aphrodite, Cadmus obtained the throne, and from the teeth of the serpent sacred to Ares he raised up the famous crop of warriors.[294]Tümpell[295] believes that the joint cult of Ares and Aphrodite originated at Thebes, and that from this city it spread through Greece, acquiring prominence in Attica and Arcadia. He finds the goddess to be the Oriental Urania, yet, strangely enough, he is unwilling to believe that she was conceived as an armed goddess in the earliest times at Thebes.

In Laconia, where Warlike Aphrodite, or Urania, was specially reverenced, the cult of Ares was more dignified and apparently more ancient than in other parts of Greece. Epicharmus is said to have claimed the deity as a Spartan.[296]Under the name Enyalius he was worshipped by the Spartan ephebes.[297]Each of the two bands into which the youths were divided sacrificed a puppy to him, performing the ceremony at night in the Phoebaeum near Therapne. The ritual bears throughout the marks of primitive times. The most striking detail is the sacrifice of dogs, in mentioning which Pausanias remarks that he knows of only one other instance, namely, to Enodia, or Hecate, at Colophon. There are, however, other records of the practice, [298] in which it is noteworthy that the custom belongs to the worship of Hecate. Ares was worshipped under his own name at Therapne in a temple which Pausanias [299] describes as one of the earliest monuments in the region. The cult legend was that the image was brought from Colchis by the Dioscuri. The god had a strange epithet, Theritas, supposedly derived from Thero, the name of his nurse. Pausanias is so dissatisfied with this etymology that he suggests that the word was learned from the Colchians and was unintelligible to the Greeks. Wide [300] states a plausible hypothesis, that the cult was of Boeotian origin, basing his theory on the affiliations of the word Theritas. It may, however, have been a very early indigenous cult, for Therapne was evidently an important pre-Dorian site, as excavations have proved. [301] Here the Dioscuri received special honours, and Helen was worshipped from old times as a nature goddess. [302] Pausanias [303] was told that the town was named from a daughter of Lelex. It is possible to infer that the cult of Ares Theritas, in which the temple was one of the oldest monuments in a region where pre-Dorian influence was strong, was "Lelegian." The people who established it would thus be akin to the Curetes of Aetolia and Acarnania. The connection with the Dioscuri favours the theory.[304]

There are two other examples of the Laconian worship of Ares. As Enyalius [305] he had a statue at Sparta near the Dromos, which represented him in fetters. In Ancient Village, a hamlet near Geronthrae, he had a sacred grove and temple. Here there was an annual festival from which women were excluded.[306]

It is, on the whole, safe to conclude that in Laconia Ares was revered in early times. The cult may have been indigenous among the pre-Dorians, or it may have been an importation from Boeotia, where he was worshipped with Aphrodite. Possibly the Fettered Ares of Sparta should be connected with a Fettered Aphrodite [307] in the same city. The two types may have given rise to a tale like that of Arcadia, of the servitude of Ares, [308] and the "lay of Demodocus" in the Odyssey could be referred to some such myth. Traditions of armed women in Tegea and in Sparta serve to connect Ares in Arcadia with Aphrodite Ἀρεία in Sparta.

There are not many traces of the cult of Ares elsewhere in Greece. The mythical genealogies of northern Greece associated him with Minyan Orchomenus, [309] Minyan Thessaly, [310] Curetis, [311] and Aetolia. [312] Mention has already been made of Thebes. At Athens [313] he was said to have been the father of Alcippe by Aglaurus, a primitive goddess. In the Peloponnese he was connected by genealogical legends with Tegea, [314] Elis, [315] and Tritea in Achaea. [316] It is impossible to give much weight to such myths unsupported by further evidence, inasmuch as there was a tendency among Greek writers of all times to consider any famous warrior of the heroic age a son of Ares. The statement applies also to warlike races like the Phlegyae, mentioned by Homer and other poets.

This investigation of the worship of Ares in Greece proper yields two important results: first, it tends to indicate that the god was worshipped in primitive times; secondly, in the relation between the cult of Ares and that of the Oriental Aphrodite at an early date in Thebes, and in the hints of a similar connection in Arcadia and Laconia, there is the suggestion of contact with the Amazons, who worshipped a goddess resembling this

Aphrodite. This raises the question whether the period may be determined in which the joint cult originated in Greek lands.

Farnell [317] conjectures that at Thebes the Oriental goddess was brought from the east by the "Cadmeans," while Ares was an ancient god of the land. He believes that "by the fiction of a marriage" her cult was reconciled to the older worship. The hostility of Cadmus toward the sacred serpent of Ares and the wrath of the god against the hero are legendary details which support some such theory as this. Cadmus seems to have been a late comer, for he is not mentioned in the Homeric poems, where Amphion and Zethus are named as the founders of Thebes. [318]It looks as if in Elis also a form of the Oriental Aphrodite was reconciled with an indigenous cult of Ares. Here the genealogical myth is not the only evidence for the worship of Ares; an altar to Ares in the race-course at Olympia attests the cult. [319]By the legend Pelops married Hippodamia, granddaughter to Ares. Hesychius [320] identifies her with Aphrodite, and Pelops, like Cadmus, was conceived as coming from the east. [321]The parallel is practically exact. In the case of Pelops the legends which connect him with Lydia and Paphlagonia are more plausibly interpreted as reflexes of Hellenic settlement in Asia Minor than as the record of the planting of an Asiatic colony near Olympia. [322]Therefore the cult of Aphrodite-Hippodamia would seem to have come into Elis by means of religious influence flowing back from the stream of emigration to the cast. Thus the Elean parallel would be of service to Farnell's argument. The Attic myth of Theseus tends, however, to support the opposite theory. This saga certainly preserved flue memory of the predominance of Crete in the Aegean. [323]Thus Aphrodite-Ariadne probably belonged to the pre-Hellenic inhabitants of Attica. It may be stated as an hypothesis that Ares was also worshipped in very early times at Athens. The evidence is this: his connection with Aglaurus, who seems to have been a primitive goddess; [324]the invocation of Ares and

Enyalius in the ephebes' oath, which associates him with Aglaurus, the Attic Charites, and Hegemone; [325]the well established cult of Ares in the fifth century on the lower slopes of the Areopagus. [326]The association with Hegemone is of special value, inasmuch as the epithet belongs to Aphrodite and to an Artemis similar to Astrateia.

The only direct information so far given concerning the worship of Ares by the Amazons comes from Athens. [327]Therefore it is reasonable to lay stress on the legend of the Oriental Aphrodite in this state [328]Yet we have no explicit statement that she was related to Ares in his capacity of patron of the Amazons. The nearest approach to a solution of the problem is possibly to be found in the ancient association between Ares and Enyo [329] Enyo was apparently identified with the armed goddess of Cappadocia who was known as Mâ, who, in turn, was identified with Cybele as Mother of the Gods. [330]Aphrodite-Ariadne and the Armed Aphrodite are in a measure forms of the Mother. Hence by an equation Aphrodite under these two types becomes identical with Enyo, the companion of Ares.

The evidence thus far gathered for a relation between Ares and the Amazons may be stated. (1) Aeschylus mentions their habitual worship of this god while they were besieging Athens; (2) Plutarch represents Theseus at this time sacrificing to Phobus, son of Ares; (3) Pausanias describes the temple of Ares at Troezen as a trophy of the victory of Theseus over the Amazons; (4) in the association between Ares and Aphrodite in several places, in similar association between Ares and Enyo, and in the identification both of this Aphrodite and of Enyo with the Mother whom the Amazons worshipped, there are obscure indications of his belonging to the rites of the Mother; (5) there are fairly good reasons for holding that Ares was an early, or pre-Hellenic god. According to this evidence it is presumable that the connection between Ares and the Amazons was indirect rather than direct. A striking fact should be added. Wherever there were memorials of the Amazons in Greece--at Athens, Troezen, Megara and Chaeronea in Boeotia, Chalcis in Euboea, [331]Thessaly [332]--there are some indications in each canton that the cult of Ares was there in early times.

There are two other sets of records which belong to the discussion of the cult of Ares in its relation to the Amazons. Of these the first is a small group of ancient references to the Amazons as children of Ares. Euripides [333]terms them Ἀρείας κόρας, a phrase echoed in the Latin Mavortia applied to one of them. [334]The term is of no value toward establishing a theory of a cult relation with Ares, for it as colourless as are the familiar epic phrases, ὄζος Ἄρηος and θεράποντες Ἄρηος, applied to warriors. Elsewhere, however, the Amazons are conceived as actually daughters of the god. The stock genealogy assigned to the race made them the children of Ares and Harmonia [335]while Otrere is individually named as the child of these parents. [336]Harmonia's name is easily associated with that of Ares, since in Theban legends she appears as his daughter. It is therefore tempting to see in the mother of the race the goddess Aphrodite. But it is impossible to follow out the clue. The relationship is manifestly a stereotyped one, manufactured by logographers. Furthermore, the mother is not consistently called Harmonia. At times she appears as Armenia [337]from which it may be inferred that the name of the mother of the Amazons came from the study of geography, and that Harmonia's crept in as a corruption. Arctinus [338] called Penthesilea a Thracian and the daughter of Ares. Possibly the theory that the race in general were children of Ares may have originated thus, or in some other poem of the Cycle. If the Amazons had not been conspicuously warriors, and if it were not at first sight a figure of speech to term a band of women the children of the war-god, it would be easier to judge whether these statements are poetical or representations of the view of genealogists.

The reference to Thrace is more valuable. Herodotus [339] shows that the cult of Ares was important here, for he says that the Thracians worshipped three gods, Ares, Dionysus, and Artemis. As it has been said, the sacrifice of dogs in the Spartan ritual of Enyalius finds its only parallels in the rites of Thracian Hecate. [340] Many modern authorities [341] believe that the cult of Ares was of Thracian origin. [342] The rites of Dionysus, to whom he was akin, [343] belong also to the orgiastic ceremonies of Phrygia. In general, as it has been noted, there is striking similarity between the cults of Phrygia and those of Thrace. This comes out strongly in the worship of the Mother. It is noteworthy that the custom of sacrificing dogs, a conspicuous and difficult feature in the rites of Ares and also of Hecate, belonged to the Carian worship of Ares. [344] It should be added that at Lagina in Caria the orgiastic worship of Hecate was established with the peculiar characteristic of the cult of Cybele at Pessinus and of Artemis at Ephesus. [345] Thus from all sides the theory finds support that the cult of Ares should be classed as Thracian-Phrygian and connected with that of the Mother. The inference is that the pre-Hellenic Ares of the Greek mainland was a god of the people who had a pre-historic culture allied to the "Minoan."

Apollonius Rhodius [346] represents the Amazons engaged in a ritual as strange as the sacrifice of dogs which suggests Thrace and Caria. He relates that on "Ares island" in Pontus they sacrificed horses in the temple of Ares. An obscure record of this is apparently preserved by the Scholiast on a line in the Lysistrata of Aristophanes. [347] The scholium mentions no deity by name; it merely comments on the legend that Amazons sacrificed horses. Ares is not elsewhere than in the passage from Apollonius named as a god thus worshipped, and possibly here, even in the temple of Ares, the ritual is to be referred rather to the worship of Cybele under baetylic form than to that of Ares. The victim was a rare one among the Greeks, belonging to Apollo, Helios, the wind-gods, and especially to Poseidon. It may be that the words of Apollonius imply a connection between the cult of Ares and that of Poseidon Hippius. At Troezen the temple of Ares gave access to the Genethlium, probably a shrine of Poseidon; [348] at Athens there was the story of the murder of Halirrhothius, son of Poseidon; [349] at Olympia the altar of Ares was dedicated to Ares Hippius. [350] The cult of Poseidon Hippius at Athens seems to have been in some way connected with that of the pre-Ionic Semnae, or Eumenides, both at Colonus Hippius and on the Areopagus. [351] Possibly the Troezenian legend of the death of Hippolytus suggests jealousy between Ares, a divinity of the Amazons, and Poseidon, the reputed father of Theseus. The ritual of horse sacrifice among the Amazons may be the basis of the tradition that they were skilful horsewomen.

The sacrifice of horses to Ares is recorded as a custom of the Scythians, [352] a people who apparently associated the horse with funerary oblations.[353]

The best example of this sacrifice in the rites of the war-god comes from Rome, [354] where on October fifteenth there was an annual race of bigae in the Campus Martius, after which the near horse of the winning pair was sacrificed to Mars, and his blood was allowed to drip on the hearth of the Regia. Probably the blood of this sacrifice was afterwards mixed with the ingredients of the sacred cakes. The rite evidently was in honour of Mars as a deity of fertility. He was undoubtedly worshipped by the primitive Romans in this capacity as well as in that of warrior. [355]

Apparently then the poetic legend of the Amazons' offering horses to Ares presents him in a very primitive aspect with the suggestion that he was a chthonic deity of fertility. As warrior and giver of increase he resembles Apollo Carneüs. A scholium [356] furnishes information which strengthens the supposition that he was in his primitive form a nature god. This tells of an obsolete custom in time of war, by which the signal for attack was given by priests of Ares called πυρφόροι, who hurled lighted torches between the two armies. This suggests the orgiastic cults of Thrace and Phrygia, in which the torch was a prominent feature. It belonged also to the ceremonies of fire in honour of Mars in primitive Rome.[357]

Even in ancient times there were conflicting theories concerning the provenience of the cult of Ares. Arnobius [358] says: "Quis Spartanum fuisse Martem (prodidit)? Non Epicharmus auctor vester? Quis is Thraciae finibus procreatum? Non Sophocles Atticus cunctis consentientibus theatris? Quis mensibus in Arcadia tribus et decem vinctum? Quis ei canes ab Caribus, quis ab Scythibus asinos immolari? Nonne principaliter cum ceteris Apollodorus?" The general tendency of the evidence is in the direction of the theory that Ares was an ancient god of the Thracians, of the pre-Hellenic peoples of Greece, and of the races who worshipped the Mother in Asia Minor and Crete.

As a god whom the Amazons worshipped he does not appear to have been as important as the Mother. The records of his association with them are few and confused. The best evidence is doubtless that furnished by the extant accounts of the saga of Theseus and the Amazons, to which Ares belongs, although it is not possible to define his position. The saga is of special importance in being analogous to the Ephesian tales of Heracles and Dionysus.

CONCLUSION

THE Amazons were votaries of Cybele, Artemis under the surnames Ephesia, Tauropolos, Lyceia, and Astrateia, Apollo called Amazonian, and Ares. The striking feature of the list is the homogeneity of its components. This is no fortuitous circumstance, for the authors from whom it has been compiled are many, and they belong to widely separated generations. The list represents classical opinion, both Greek and Latin, on the nature of the divinities whom the Amazons were conceived to have served. It must be concluded that these women were associated with the cults of primitive deities of fertility and of war, among whom a Woman was the chief figure, and of whom the rites were orgiastic. In historical times such cults may be classed as Thracian-Phrygian, and they are to be referred to the people who inherited both the blood and the spiritual traditions of the great pre-historic civilisation of the Aegean basin, of which the brilliant centre seems to have been Crete.

The theories concerning the Amazons which have commanded most respect are three: (1) that the tradition arose from memories of the raids of warlike women of the Cimmerians and kindred peoples, who in early times forced their way into Asia Minor from the north; (2) that the Amazons were originally the warrior-priestesses, or hieroduli, of the Hittite-Cappadocian Mâ, and that the Hittites passed on legends about them to the people of Lycia, Lydia, and adjoining lands; (3) that the tradition of the Amazons was grounded on the mistaken notion, deeply rooted among the Greeks, that beardlessness is a sure indication of female sex, whence they failed to recognise as men certain warriors who appeared at an early date as foes of the people of Asia Minor. To the first [359] of these it is to be objected--irrespective of evidence furnished by the cults with which the Amazons were associated--that a northern home beyond the Euxine was assigned to the race by Aeschylus and Herodotus, but that the oldest records of the Greeks, the Homeric poems, place them near Lycia and Phrygia. In this region the tradition struck down into the soil, as shown by the tales of many cities claiming the Amazons as their founders. To the second [360] it must be replied that Mâ is nowhere named in direct connection with the Amazons, although she resembles in a general way the female deities whom they were said to have worshipped. Furthermore, in the records of her rites there is no hint of armed hieroduli. [361] And, still further, the evidence on which the assumption rests that the Hittite kingdom was one of great importance and influence is not strong. The last theory [362] is very interesting, because it is novel and daring, and also because it draws attention to certain curious facts usually overlooked by anthropologists. But as a foundation for the persistent tradition of the Amazons as armed women it is too slight in structure.

The tradition, interpreted in the light of evidence furnished by the cults which they are supposed to have practised, seems to have originated among the people who built up the prehistoric civilisation of the Aegean, of which the finished product was apparently "Minoan" culture. In their warlike character the Amazons are reflexes of the Woman whom they worshipped. Like the Warrior Goddess of Asia Minor they carry the battle-axe, and in this they are shown to be closely related to the religion of pre-historic Crete, of which the weapon is the conspicuous symbol. Their other weapon, the bow, is also Cretan. [363] It is the attribute of the Asiatic-Cretan Apollo whom they seem to have revered. They belong to the early matriarchate, which left traces in Caria and Lycia.[364] In Greece itself, even in Laconia, the canton belonging to the fiercest of the Hellenic invaders who introduced the patriarchate, women enjoyed unusual freedom in Greek times, and here there were stories of their having borne arms for their country. There were similar tales at Argos and in Arcadia, and at the Olympian Heraeum there was a footrace of maidens in honour of Hippodamia.[365] These are doubtless vestiges of the matriarchate of the pre-Hellenic inhabitants of Greece. They suggest many comparisons with the Amazon tradition. The legend of Atalanta offers similar parallels to the story of the Amazons in its pleasing aspect. Its darker side, which the older Greeks emphasised, is reflected in the tale of the Lemnian women who murdered their husbands.[366] These were Myrina's children and descendants of Dionysus. The energy of this ancient matriarchal organisation is shown in the idea of confusion of sex which belonged to the cults of Cybele and Ephesian Artemis in historical times. The idea is prominent in the legends of the Amazons, as they touch religion. At Ephesus they were connected with Dionysus and Heracles, to both of whom an effeminate character belonged. Their place in state cult at Athens has the same implications.

We may believe then that the tradition of the Amazons preserves memories of a time when women held the important place in state and religion in Aegean lands, and that they reflect the goddess of this civilisation. It is noteworthy that the earliest writings of the Greeks concerning them show them in that part of Asia Minor where the rites of the Mother throughout ancient times menaced the reason of her worshippers. The troop of maenads who followed Dionysus were like the Amazons, but the clue to their kinship was easily lost.[367] The relationship between the Amazons and the Anatolian cults was practically obliterated, whereas maenads were introduced into Greek religion after many generations had altered the first form of orgiastic worship. Moreover, the deity of the maenads, who was earlier only the paredros of the Woman, had become an Olympian.

Greek travellers of the age of Herodotus naturally inferred that they had discovered the Amazons in the regions of Scythia and Libya where armed women were said to fight in the ranks with men. Even before this time the traditional home of the race had been placed further and further eastward, as Greek colonists failed to find Amazons in Lydia, Phrygia, Lycia, and along the southern shore of the Euxine. Yet, granted the origin of the Amazon tradition among the "Minoans" and their kindred, it is at present impossible to say that these pre-historic races had no affiliations with Scythians, Libyans, and Hittites.

BIBLIOGRAPHY

BERGMANN, F. G. Les Amazones dans l'histoire et dans la fable. Colmar. Undated.

Bethe, E. Article on the Minos Legends. Rheinisches Museum, Vol. 65, 1910.

British School Annual, Vol. 14, 1907-08; Vol. 15, 1908-09; Vol. 16, 1909-10. Reports of Excavations in Sparta.

Burrows, R. M. Discoveries in Crete. London, 1907.

Cook, A. B. Animal Worship in the Mycenaean Age. Journal of Hellenic Studies, 1894.

Corey, A. D. De Amazonum Antiquissimis Figuris. Berlin, 1891.

Daremberg et Saglio (and later E. Pottier). Dictionnaire des antiquités grecques et romaines. Paris. In progress of publication.

Dawkins, R. Survival of the Dionysus Cult in Thrace. Journal of Hellenic Studies, 1906.

Dörpfeld, W. Troja und Ilion. Athens, 1901.

Evans, A. Discoveries in Crete. Reports in British School Annual, Vols. 6-10, 1899-1904, and Journal of Hellenic Studies, Vol. 21, 1901.

Fairbanks, A. Handbook of Greek Religion. New York, 1911.

Farnell, L. R. Cults of the Greek States. 5 vols. Oxford, 1896-1909. Sociological Hypotheses concerning the position of women in Ancient Religion. Archiv für Religionswissenschaft, 1904.

Fowler, W. W. Lustratio. An essay published in R. R. Marett's Anthropology and the Classics. Oxford, 1908.

Frazer, J. G. Golden Bough (The). 3d edition. 5 parts.

Part 1. The Magic Art and the Evolution of Kings. London, 1906.

Part 2. The Perils of the Soul and the Doctrine of Taboo. London, 1906.

Part 4. Attis, Adonis: Osiris. A Comparative Study in Oriental Religion. London, 1907.

Pausanias. Description of Greece. 6 vols. London, 1898.

Guhl, E. K. Ephesiaca. Berlin, 1843.

Hall, H. R. Oldest Civilisation in Greece. London and Philadelphia, 1901.

Harrison, J. E. Hera and Zeus. Classical Review, 1893.

Prolegomena to the Study of Greek Religion. Cambridge, 1903.

Hymn of the Kouretes. Discussed jointly with R. C. Bosanquet and G. Murray, British School Annual, Vol. 15, 1908-09.

Mythology and Monuments of Ancient Athens. Published jointly with K. Verrall. London and New York, 1890.

Hawes, C. H. and H. B. Crete, the Forerunner of Greece. London and New York, 1909.

Hawes, H. B. Gournia, Vasiliki, and other Prehistoric Sites on the Isthmus of Hierapetra, Crete. Philadelphia, 1909.

Hogarth, D. G. Inscriptions and Other Antiquities of Hierapolis Syriae. British School Annual, Vol. 14, 1907-08.

Ionia and the East. London, 1909.

The Hittites. Journal of the Royal Anthropological Institute, Vol. 39, 1910.

Imhoof-Blumer, F. Amazons on Greek Coins. Nomisma, Vol. 2, 1909.

Kern, O. Article on the Samothracian Mysteries. Archäologischer Anzeiger, 1893.

Klügmann, O. Über die Amazonen der kleinasiatischen Städte. Philologus, Vol. 25, 1870.

Leonhard, W. Hettiter und Amazonen. Die griechische Tradition über die Chatti und ein Versuch zu ihrer historischen Verwertung. Leipzig, 1911.

Mencke, T. Lydiaca. Leipzig, 1813.

Mordtmann, A. D. Die Amazonen. Hannover, 1862.

Moreau de Jonnés, A. C. L'Océan des anciens et les peuples préhistoriques. Paris, 1873.

Mosso, A. Palaces of Crete and their Builders. London and New York, 1907.

Müller, O. Orchomenos und die Minyer. 2 vols. 2d ed. Berlin, 1844.

Murray, G. Rise of the Greek Epic. London, 1907.

Myres, J. L. Herodotus and Anthropology. An essay published in R. R. Marett's Anthropology and the Classics. Oxford, 1908.

History of the Pelasgian Theory. Journal of Hellenic Studies, Vol. 27, 1907.

Nagel, F. Geschichte der Amazonen. Stuttgart, 1838.

Pauly-Wissowa. Real-encyklopädie der klassischen Altertumswissenschaft. Stuttgart, 1894-1910.

Perrot et Chipiez. Histoire de l'art dans l'antiquité. Vols. 1-6. Paris, 1882-1894.

Petersen, E. Ercole e le Amazons. Annali dell' Instituto, Vol. 56, 1884.

Pinches, T. G. The Goddess Ištar in Assyro-Babylonian Literature. Proceedings of the Society of Biblical Archaeology, Vol. 31, 1909.

Preller-Robert. Griechische Mythologie. 4th ed. Berlin, 1907.

Prinz, H. Article on Minoan Religion. Athenische Mitteilungen, Vol. 35, 1910.

Radet, G. Cybébé. Etude sur les transformations plastiques d'un type divin. Bordeaux, 1909.

Reinach, A. J. Une Amazone Hétéenne. Revue Archéologique, Vol. 16, 1910.

Reinach, S. Orpheus. Histoire générale des religions. 3d ed. Paris, 1909.

Ridgeway, W. Early Age of Greece. 2 vols. Cambridge, 1900.

Article on same subject. Journal of Hellenic Studies Vol. 16, 1896.

Roscher, W. H. Ausführliches Lexikon der griechischen und ramischen Mythologie. Leipzig, 1884- Incomplete.

Rouse, W. H. D. Greek Votive Offerings. London, 1902.

Sayce, A. H. The Discoveries at Boghaz Keui in Cappadocia. Biblical World, Vol. 33, 1909.

The Figure of an Amazon from Boghaz Keui. Proceedings of the Society of Biblical Archaeology, Vol. 32, 1910.

Smith, Cecil. An article on the Horse. Journal of Hellenic Studies, Vol. 10, 1890.

Stengel, P. Article on Horse Sacrifice. Archiv für Religionswissenschaft, 1905.

Stricker, W. Die Amazonen in Sage und Geschichte. Berlin, 1868.

Sybel, L. von. Weltgeschichte der Kunst in Altertum. Marburg, 1900- ------. Incomplete.

Tümpel, K. Ares und Aphrodite. Fleckeisen's Jahrbücher für Philologie und Pädagogik, Suppl. 11, 1880.

Article on Gynaecocracy. Philologus, 1892.

Verrall, A. W. Death and the Horse. Journal of Hellenic Studies, Vol. 18,1898.

Voigt, F. A. Beiträge zur Mythologie des Ares und der Athena. Wiener Studien, 1881.

Welcker, F. G. Der epische Cyclus. Bonn, 1835.

Griechische Götterlehre. 3 vols. Göttingen, 1857-62.

Wright, J. H. Worship of Mâ; Μήν. Harvard Studies in Classical Philology, Vol. 6.

ENDNOTES

[1] Iliad, 6. 168-195. (p. 1)

[2] Ibid. 3. 182-190. (p. 1)

[3] Ibid. 6.186. (p. 1)

[4] Ibid. 2. 811-815. (p. 2)

[5] Cf. Diod. Sic. 3. 54, 55; Strabo, 12. 573; 13. 623; Plato, Cratyl. 392a; Schol. Oppian, Halieutica, 3. 403; Hesych. s.v. βατίεια and s. κάρθμοιο Μυρίνης; Eust. ad D. Per. 828. (p. 2)

[6] Save for one unimportant version (Dar. Phryg.), wherein Penthesilea is slain by Pyrrhus, son of Achilles, her death by the hand of her lover Achilles is a regular convention in Greek literature. Cf. Q. Sm. l. 19 ff., 134; Nonnus, 35. 28; Hellan, in Tzetz. Post-Hom. 19; Et. M. 493, 41; Lycoph. 997; Diet. Cret. 3. 15; 4. 2; Eust. Hom. 1696, 52; Hyg. Fab. 112, 225; Serv. ad Aen. l. 491; Just. 2. 4; Ovid, Her. 21. 118; Prop. 3. 9, 14. For evidence concerning the treatment of the subject in Greek painting see Paus. 5. 11, 6. (p. 3)

[7] Diod. Sic. 2. 46. (p. 3)

[8] St. Basil, s.v. Ἀλόπη. (p. 3)

[9] Cf. Ap. Rh. 2. 389 and Schol. Tzetz. Post-Hom. 8. 189; Schol. Ap. Rh. 2. 1032; Schol. Iliad, 3. 189; Lyc. Cass. 997; Hyg. Fab. 30, 112, 163, 223, 225. (p. 3)

[10] Pherec. ap. Schol. Ap. Rh. 2. 992; Lys. 2. 4; Isoc. 4. 68; 12. 193; Nonnus, 34. 158. For a discussion of the bearing of this fact see Chapter V. (p. 3)

[11] Welcker (Der epische Cyclus, 2. pp. 200 ff.) derives the lines from the Atthis or Amazonides of Hegesinus, a writer for whom the only extant source is Pausanias, 9. 29, 1 ff. Lübbert, however (De Pindari Studiis Hesiodeis et Homericis, pp. 10 ff.), derives them from the Eoeae of Hesiod, an opinion which Rzach follows (ed. of Hesiod, p. 197). A third theory is advanced by Corey (De Amazonum Antiquissimis Figuris, p. 42), namely, that the fragment is from the work of Cynaethus (circa 504 B.C.). On the chance that it is older than Corey believes, the fragment should be considered along with the data which may be collected about the Amazons from the literature of the centuries immediately following Homer. (p. 4)

[12] Robert (Hermes, 19. pp. 485 ff.) conjectures a single epic, the Amazonika by Onasus, as the source of the accounts of the expedition of Heracles and Telamon given by Pindar in three places, Nemean, 3. 36 ff.; 4. 25 ff.; Isthmian, 6 (5). 27 ff. He dates this lost epic before the sixth century B.C. Corey (op. cit. pp. 35 ff.) finds evidence for two epic accounts, the first epitomised by Hellanicus (Fr. 33, 136, 138 in Müller, Frag. Hist. Graec. 1. pp. 49-64), the second given by Apollodorus (Bibl. 2. 5, 9, 7-12; 6. 4-7, 1). (p. 4)

[13] On Heracles and Hippolyta cf. Plut. Thes. 37; Paus. 1. 41, 7; Ap. Rh. 2. 781 and Schol. 1001; Nonn. 25. 251; Q. Sm. 1. 24; 6. 242; Planud, Anthol. 91; Isocr. 12. 193; Apollod. 2. 5, 9; Diod. Sic. 2. 46, 416; Plut. Quaest. Gr. 45; Pherec. ap. Athen. 13. 557, 9; Arrian, Anab. 7. 13, 5; Luc. Anach. 34; Zen. 5. 33; Et. M. 1 402, 13. (p. 4)

[14] On Theseus and Antiope cf. Paus. 5. 11, 4-5; Plut. Thes. 26 (from Philochorus); Isocr. Panath. 193; Plut. Thes. (quoting Theseid); Pindar ap. Paus. 1. 2, 1; Pherec. ap. Plut. Thes. 26; Schol. Pind. Nem. 5. 89; Plut. (Thes. 27) and Euripides (Hippolytus) name this Amazon Hippolyta. (p. 5)

[15] On the authority of Welcker most scholars consider the Nosti of Agias or Hegias the epic source for the tales of Theseus and Antiope. (p. 5)

[16] Paus. 1. 2, 1. (p. 5)

[17] For a good statement of the general attitude in ancient times on this question of the reality of the Amazons see Strabo, 11. p. 505. According to Lysias (Epitaph. 3) the race of the Amazons was almost exterminated in the invasion of Attica. Cf. Isocr. Panegyr. p. 206; Demosth. Epitaph.; Plato, Menex. 9; De Legg. 2. p. 804. (p. 6)

[18] Tomb of Antiope at Athens, Paus. 1. 2, 1; cf. Pseudo-Plato, Axioch. pp. 364a-365a. Tomb of Hippolyta at Megara, Paus. 1. 41, 7; cf. Plut. Thes. 27. Tomb of Amazons at Chaeronea and in Thessaly, Plut. Thes. 28. Tomb of Myrina near Troy, Iliad, 2. 811, and schol. and Eust. ad l: cf. Strabo, 12. 573; 13. 623. Tomb of Anaea the city of that name, Steph. Byz. s.v. Ἀναία (quoting Ephorus). Tomb of Penthesilea, Aristeas, ep. 5 (Bergk, 1900). (p. 6)

[19] Paus. 1. 41, 7. (p. 6)

[20] Herod. 9. 27. (p. 6)

[21] Strabo, 2. 126. (p. 6)

[22] Diod. Sic. 3. 52 ff. (p. 7)

[23] Cf. Diod. Sic. 3. 66. (p. 7)

[24] There were two other cities in Asia Minor named Myrina. All three were connected with the name of the Amazon, but among them the city of Aeolis seems to take precedence. Cf. Eust. ad Dion. Per. 828. 5; Schol. Iliad, 2. 814; Diod. Sic. 3. 54, 55; Strabo, 12. 573; 13. 623. (p. 7)

[25] Cf. Klügmann, Über die Amazonen der kleinasiatischen Städte, in Philologus, 30. pp. 529 ff. These cities were Ephesus, Smyrna, Cyme, Paphos, and Sinope. (p. 7)

[26] Cf. especially coins of Smyrna. (p. 7)

[27] Anon. St. Mar. M. 283. (p. 7)

[28] Plin. N. H. 4. 12. (p. 7)

[29] Nic. Dam. Fr. 62. (p. 7)

[30] The story that Penthesilea bore to Achilles a child Caÿster is probably too late to be of any value to this discussion. (p. 7)

[31] As it has been stated (p. 6), this is the geographical theory of the Cycle. It should be added that Hecataeus, who associates Sinope on the Euxine with the Amazons (Fr. 352), and Mela, who mentions a city Amazonium in Pontus (1. 19; cf. Plin. N. H. 6. 4), are probably to be classed with the non-epic sources who follow the theory. (p. 8)

[32] Herod. 4. 110-117. (p. 8)

[33] The Amazons are often styled Maeotides. Cf. Mela, 1. 1; Justin, 2. 1; Curt. 5. 4; Lucan, 2; Ovid, Fasti, 3; El. 12; Ep. Sab. 2. 9; Verg. Aen. 6. 739.
In discussing the geography of this region about Lake Maeotis, a note is called for on the confusion which Pape finds (Wörterbuch, s.v. Ἀμαζών) between Ἀλαζῶνες and Ἀμαζῶνες. It would seem that the former is a misspelling for the latter, appearing in Strabo's quotation from Ephorus (12. 550). That the masculine article is used with it does not seem odd, if one recalls St. Basil's statement (s.v. Ἀμαζών), that the word may stand in the masculine. Herodotus mentions (4. 17, 52) a folk called Ἀλιζῶνες, whose country lay on the northeast shore of the Euxine, but these are not Amazons. (p. 8)

[34] Herod. 4. 102 ff. (p. 8)

[35] Herod. 4. 117. (p. 8)

[36] V. supra, pp. 1 and 4. (p. 8)

[37] Prom. V. 707-735. (p. 9)

[38] Strabo, p. 492. (p. 9)

[39] Herod. 4. 19. (p. 9)

[40] Herod. 1. 28. (p. 9)

[41] Strabo, p. 678. (p. 9)

[42] Prom. V. 415-419. (p. 9)

[43] Supplices, 287. (p. 9)

[44] Strabo, 7, p. 300. (p. 9)

[45] Strabo, p. 505. (p. 9)

[46] As the Greeks travelled more, there was a growing tendency among them to place the original home of the Amazons further and further away. As they did not find such a folk in western Asia Minor, or along the southern shore of the Euxine, it was natural for them to suppose that they were to be sought in the little explored regions of Scythia, also of Libya. Such reasoning was reinforced by reports which came of Scythian and Libyan women who were warriors. (p. 10)

[47] Paus. 1. 2, 1; Diod. Sic. 4. 28, 2, 3; Clitod, ap. Plut. Thes. 27; Isaeus ap. Harpocration; Suidas, s.v. Ἀμαζόνειον. (p. 10)

[48] Paus. 2. 31, 4-5. (p. 10)

[49] Paus. 1. 41, 7; Plut. Thes. 27. (p. 10)

[50] Plut. Thes. 28. (p. 10)

[51] Plut. Thes. 37, 3. (p. 10)

[52] Plut. Thes. 28. (p. 10)

[53] Schol. and Eust. ad Iliad, 3. 189; Diod. Sic. 2. 45; Justin, 2. 4, 5; Apollod. 2. 5, 9; Arrian, Anab. 7. 13, 2. Cf. Latin Unimammia of Plautus, Curcul. 3. 75. (p. 10)

[54] Hippocr. De Acre Locis et Aquis, 17. Herodotus seems to have been the first to speak of the Sarmatians as descendants of the Amazons (4. 110-117). In this he was followed by Ephorus (Fr. 103); Scymn. Chius, 5. 102; Plato, De Legg. 7. p. 804; Diod. Sic. 2. 34. (p. 10)

[55] Philostr. Heroïd. 20. 42. (p. 10)

[56] Cf. Plin. N. H. 34. 75. (p. 12)

[57] In the Mattei type the left breast is bare, in the Capitoline, the right. In the Berlin type and in that in Lansdowne House the left breast is entirely bare, and the right is almost entirely so. (p. 12)

[58] Paus. 1. 25, 2; Plut. Anton. 60; S. Q. 1995, 1996. (p. 12)

[59] Xen. ap. Pollux, 1. 134; Plin. N. H. 3. 43; Paus. 1. 41, 7. (p. 12)

[60] Paus. 10. 31, 8. (p. 12)

[61] The double-axe is called σάγαρις (securis) and also πέλεκυς. Cf. Xen. Anab. 4. 4; Q. Sm. 1. 597. Plutarch (Pomp. 35) mentions the axe and the pelta as Amazonian arms. The latter was carried also by the Thracians and Persians. (p. 12)

[62] Paus. 10. 31, 8. (p. 12)

[63] Corey tabulates the types which he finds in vase-painting, op. cit. pp. 49 ff. (p. 13)

[64] Cf. e. g. Paus. 1. 15, 2; 10. 31, 8. Cf. Frazer, Paus. 2. 139. (p. 13)

[65] Livy, 29. 10, 11. (p. 14)

[66] Apollon. Argon. 2. 1172-1177. Because of its resemblance to the Black Stone of Pessinus, it seems impossible to interpret the stone mentioned by Apollonius otherwise than as the symbol of Cybele, although it was placed in a temple of Ares. For the view that it represented Ares v. H. de La Ville do Mirmont, La Mythologie et les Dieux dans les Argonautiques et dans l'Énéide, Paris, 1894, p. 569. V. infra, n. 346. (p. 14)

[67] Diod. Sic. 3. 55. (p. 14)

[68] Apollod. 3. 12; Diod. Sic. 4. (p. 14)

[69] Strabo, 10. pp. 469, 472; 12. p. 567. Cf. Hor. Carm. 1. 16, 5; Catull. Atys, 63. (p. 15)

[70] Diod. Sic. 5. 64. (p. 15)

[71] Hyg. Poet. 2. 4. (p. 15)

[72] Strabo, 10. pp. 469, 572; 12. p. 567; 14. pp. 640-641; Diod. Sic. 3. 58; Mar. Par. ap. C. Müller, Fr. 1. 544; Ovid, Fasti, 1. 237, 363; Plin. N. H. 5. 147; 11. 261; 31. 9; 35. 165; Catull. Atys. Cf. Anthol. Pal. 7. 217-220. (p. 15)

[73] Paus. 7. 17, 10-12. (p. 15)

[74] Strabo (12. p. 567) says that Cretan Rhea received the name Agdistis at Pessinus, and that on Mt. Agdistis near this city the tomb of Atys was shown. Cf. Paus. 1. 4, 5. (p. 16)

[75] Paus. 7. 17, 9-10. (p. 16)

[76] For a complete treatise on Atys cf. Frazer, Attis, Adonis: Osiris, in Golden Bough, Part 4. (p. 16)

[77] The idea was revolting to the Greeks. Cf. Herod. 3. 48; 8. 105; Aristot. Polit. 5. 8, 12. The practice was common among the Phrygians and other Asiatics of ancient times. With Herod. S. 105 cf. Soph. Fr. from Troilus ap. Pollux, 10. 165. As a religious detail it belonged to the rites of Artemis at p. 20 Ephesus, to those of Zeus and Hecate at Lagina in Caria, to those of Aphrodite at Bambyce, or Hierapolis, in Syria. In each of these instances the deity partakes in some measure of the characteristics of Cybele. Cf. Farnell, Cults of the Greek States, 2. pp. 506 ff., p. 590. (p. 16)

[78] Hesiod. Theog. 161; Schol. Ap. Rh. 1129 (quoting Phoronis); Strabo, 10. p. 472. (p. 16)

[79] The story of the overthrow of Uranus belongs to the Hesiodic theogony (Hes. Theog. 160, 182). It has a counterpart in the later Orphic theogony, in the story of the overthrow of Cronus by Zeus. Both myths centre about the Dictaean Cave in Crete. The worship of Dictaean Zeus seems to have belonged to the Eteocretans (Strabo, 10. p. 478). (p. 16)

[80] Lucr. De Rerum Natura, 2. 600-640. (p. 16)

[81] Catull. Atys, ad finem. (p. 17)

[82] Photius and Suidas s.v. μητραγύρτης. These priests find a strikingly exact counterpart in the howling dervishes of Mohammedanism. In fact, many close parallels to the worship of the Great Mother may be met in the Orient to-day. The word Cybebus is evidently the masculine form of the name of the goddess, given by Herodotus as Κυβήβη (Herod. 5. 102). (p. 17)

[83] Juv. Sat. 6. 512 ff. (p. 17)

[84] The two deities were so completely blended into one that even in early Greek writings it was needless to discriminate between them. Cf. the complete identification of Rhea with Cybele in the Homeric Hymn to the Mother of the Gods (14). (p. 17)

[85] Paus. 8. 37, 6. (p. 17)

[86] The Κουρήτων and Κοβυβάντων γένεσις of Epimenides, referred to in Strabo, 10. p. 474, and Diog. Laert. 1. 10. (p. 17)

[87] In the course of excavations at Palaikastro in Crete a hymn of the Curetes was discovered, which is dated about 300 B.C. The hymn is discussed in three papers, British School Annual, 15 (1908-09): (1) Miss J. E. Harrison (pp. 308-338), "The Kouretes and Zeus Kouros: A Study in Pre-historic Sociology"; (2) R. C. Bosanquet (pp. 339-356), Text of the Hymn and certain religious aspects, "The Cult of Diktaean Zeus" and "The Cult of the Kouretes"; (3) Gilbert Murray (pp. 356-365), Restored Text, Translation, and Commentary. Miss Harrison's study is under these headings: "1. The Kouretes as Δαίμονες and Πρόπολοι; 2. The Kouretes as Magicians, as Μάντεις and Metallurgists; 3. The Kouretes as armed Ὀρχηστῆρες; 4. The Kouretes as Φύλακες and Παιδοτρόφοι; 5. Zagreus and the Thunder-Rites; 6. The Kouros as Year-God; 7. The Kouretes as Ὀργιοφάνται." The three articles form a very valuable contribution to the study of orgiastic cults and kindred subjects. (p. 17)

[88] Farnell speaks with certainty (op. cit. 2. p. 306) of the primitive warlike character of Cybele. (p. 18)

[89] Hesiod. Theog. 452, 487; Apollod. 1. 1, 6. The Orphic theogony connects the shouts of the Curetes and the clashing of their shields with the story of the overthrow of Cronus by Zeus. Cf. Lobeck, Aglaoph. p. 519; Hermann, Orphica, 6. p. 456. (p. 18)

[90] Paus. 5. 7, 6. The scholiast on the passage says that they were ten in number. Paus. gives the same names for the five, 5. 14, 7. (p. 18)

[91] Paus. 10. 38, 7. (p. 18)

[92] On Idas and Lynceus cf. Pind. Nem. 10. 55-90; Paus. 4. 3, 1. (p. 18)

[93] Hes. Theog. 970; Verg. Aen. 3. 168. (p. 18)

[94] Paus. 5. 7, 6; 5. 14, 9. (p. 18)

[95] Paus. 9. 27, 6-8. (p. 18)

[96] Diod. Sic. 5. 154; Hes. Theog. 970. (p. 18)

[97] Herod. 2. 51. (p. 18)

[98] Herod. 3. 37. (p. 19)

[99] Cf. Journ. Hellen. Studies, 13. pl. 4; Athenische Mitteilungen (1888), pl. 9-12. (p. 19)

[100] Paus. 9. 25, 5-6. (p. 19)

[101] Welcker, Aeschyl. Trilogie, pp. 161-211. He connects the word with καίειν. (p. 19)

[102] Pindar, Isth. 6. 3. (p. 19)

[103] Cf. Homeric Hymn, 14. 3-4. (p. 19)

[104] On the Phrygian character of the music used in the worship of Dionysus, cf. Aristot. Polit. 8. 7, 9. Euripides in the Bacchae completely identifies the rites of Dionysus with the Phrygian worship of the Mother. Cf. especially lines 58 ff. Euripides in the Helena, 1320 ff., assigns to Demeter all the attributes of Rhea. Apollodorus tells (3. 5, 1) that Dionysus, driven mad by Hera, was cured by Rhea at Cybela in Phrygia, and that he received from her woman's attire. (p. 19)

[105] On the worship of Cybele in Lydia cf. Herod. 5. 102; Paus. 7. 17, 9-10. An epitaph by Callimachus (Epigram. 42, p. 308, ed. Ernst) illustrates the general resemblance of one orgiastic cult to another. This tells of a priestess who had served Demeter of Eleusis, the Cabiri, and, finally, Cybele. Cf. also the history of the Metroüm at Athens, which was in earlier times a temple of Eleusinian Demeter (Arrian, A.

O; Hesych. s.v. Εὐδάνεμος; Dion. Hal. Dein. 11. p. 658, 3), but served later as temple of the Mother of the Gods, of whom Phidias, or Agoracritus, made the statue with tympanum and lions as attributes (Arrian, Peripl. 9; Paus. 1. 3, 5; Plin. N. H. 36. 17; Aesch. 1. 60; Diog. Laert. 6. 2, 3; Epistol. Gr. p. 239; Photius and Suidas s. v. μητραγύρτης. (p. 19)

[106] Diod. Sic. 3. 55. (p. 20)

[107] Kern holds (Arch. Anz. 1893, p. 130) that in the statement of Diodorus there is no proved connection between the Amazons and the mysteries of Samothrace. (p. 20)

[108] Paus. 7. 4, 3. (p. 20)

[109] Cf. ch. III on Ephesian Artemis. (p. 20)

[110] Schol. Aristoph. Pax, 276. (p. 20)

[111] Ovid, Trist. 1, el. 9. 19; Liv. 38. 41. (p. 20)

[112] V. supra, n. . (p. 20)

[113] Strabo, p. 473. Cf. rites of Artemis-Hecate, Orph. Argon. 905. (p. 20)

[114] Farnell, op. cit. 2. pp. 504 ff. (p. 20)

[115] Sext. Empir. (Bekker), 174. (p. 21)

[116] Strabo, p. 466: ὥστε καὶ τὰ ἱερὰ τρόπον τινὰ κοινοποιεῖσθαι ταῦτά τε (referring to the Corybantic rites Of Crete) καὶ τῶν Σαμοθρᾴκων καὶ τὰ ἐν Λήμνῳ. (p. 21)

[117] Hesych. s.v. Δίλογχος. (p. 21)

[118] Schol. Plato, Republic, 327. Cf. Mommsen, Heort. p. 488. (p. 21)

[119] An inscription from Byzantium (Mordtmann u. Déthier, Epig. v. Byz. Taf. 6-8) reads: Μηρτὶ Θεῶν Μᾶ Cf. Steph. Byz. s.v. Μάσταυρα; Strabo, pp. 535, 537; Paus. 3. 16, 8; Dio Cass. 36B. Cf. article by J. H. Wright, Harv. Studies in Class. Philol. 6. 64, on the worship of Mâ; Μήν. (p. 21)

[120] Paus. 2. 30, 3. (p. 21)

[121] Pseudo-Lucian, De Dea Syria. The torch belonged to her festival (op. cit. 49). (p. 21)

[122] Pausanias (3. 16, 8) identifies Artemis Taurica, Artemis Brauronia, and the goddess of Laodicea in Syria. He also says that the original image of this cult was claimed by the Laodiceans, the Cappadocians, the neighbours of the latter on the borders of the Euxine, the Lydians--who called it Anaiitis--, the Spartans--who called it Orthia. (p. 21)

[123] Cf. ch. III, Ephesian Artemis. (p. 21)

[124] Paus. 7. 6, 6. (p. 21)

[125] Diod. Sic. 2. 46. (p. 21)

[126] Arnob. Adv. Nat. 5. 7. (p. 21)

[127] This comes out strongly in the rites at Bambyce. V. supra, n. . (p. 22)

[128] Cf. Strabo, 10. pp. 469, 472; 12. p. 567, wherein the names associated with the cult are traced to Phrygian localities. Diod. Sic. (3. 58) derives the name of the goddess from a place in Phrygia. On Cybele in Lydia cf. Herod. 5. 102; Paus. 7. 17, 9-10. (p. 22)

[129] Strabo, 10. p. 478. V. supra, n. . (p. 22)

[130] Klügmann, op. cit. p. 529. (p. 22)

[131] Herod. 2. 51. (p. 22)

[132] For the views of Herodotus on the Pelasgi cf. 2. 56-58; 7. 94: 8. 44. J. L. Myres has an important article, "The History of the Pelasgian Theory," in Journ. Hellen. Studies, 27 (1907). (p. 22)

[133] Paus. 7. 4, 3. (p. 22)

[134] The central point of the mysteries of Samothrace seems to have been the worship of Demeter as the mother of Plutus. It is interesting to note that this son was born in Crete (Hes. Theog. 970). (p. 22)

[135] Cf. Herod. 4. 103 and the conception of the goddess on which Euripides builds his Iphigeneia among the Taurians. Possibly the word Ταυρόπολος is to be connected with Taurobolium, the mystic baptism in blood, which was originally connected with Syrian cults, especially with that of Mithras. In the first half of the second century A.D. it was introduced at Rome as a feature of the worship of Magna Mater. On the Taurobolia and the similar Criobolia cf. Prudent. Peristeph. 10. 1011-1050. (p. 23)

[136] On the history of the Artemisium cf. Plin. N. H. 36. 14; Mela, 1. 17; Ptol. 5; Plut. Alex. (p. 24)

[137] This is Pliny's story (N. H. 34. 53). Students of Greek art are not unanimous in believing that four statues were executed. For a well arranged bibliography on the question cf. Overbeck, Gesch. d. griech. Plastik, 1. pp. 514 ff. and Notes, p. 527. (p. 24)

[138] Tac. Annales, 3. 61. (p. 24)

[139] Thuc. 3. 104. (p. 24)

[140] Herod. 1. 142, 146. Cf. Paus. 7. 2, 1-4. (p. 25)

[141] Herod. 1. 147. On the Apaturia cf. Ephor. ap. Harpocr. s.v.; Strabo, 9. p. 393. (p. 25)

[142] The Codrids were refugees who sought shelter at Athens, having been driven out of the Peloponnese by the Dorians (Paus. 7. 1, 9). (p. 25)

[143] Strabo, 12 and 14. Cf. Paus. 7. 2, 6 ff. (p. 25)

[144] Paus. 7. 2, 9. (p. 25)

[145] Paus. 7. 2, 6-8. (p. 25)

[146] Herodotus (5. 100) gives Coressus as a place-name in Ephesus. (p. 25)

[147] ἄσυλον δὲ μένει τὸ ἱερὸν καὶ νῦν καὶ πρότερον (Strabo, p. 641). The shrine of Aphrodite Stratonikis at Smyrna was also a place of asylum. Neither Aphrodite nor Artemis appears in such capacity in purely Hellenic cults. (p. 26)

[148] Et. Mag. 402. 20. (p. 26)

[149] Pind. ap. Paus. 7. 2, 7. (p. 26)

[150] Callim. in Dian. 237 ff. (p. 26)

[151] The Greek is φηγῷ ὑπ᾽ εὐπρέμνῳ. The words hardly bear Farnell's construction (op. cit. 2. p. 482), "in the trunk of a tree." (p. 26)

[152] Just. 2. 4. So also Hyg. Fab. 237. Cf. St. Basil (s.v. Ἔφεσος) and Eust, (ad Dion. 823), who give Ἀμαζώ as daughter of Ephesus and mother of the Amazons. Cf. Cram. A. 0. 1. 80. (p. 26)

[153] Paus. 7. 2, 7-8. (p. 26)

[154] Tac. l. c. (Ann. 3. 61). (p. 26)

[155] Paus. 4. 31, 8. (p. 27)

[156] Artemid. Oneirocr. 4. 4. Cf., however, Aristoph. Nub. 599-600. (p. 27)

[157] On the statue cf. Aristoph. Nub. 590; Aelian, Hist. Animal. 12. 9; Strabo. 12. p. 534; 13. p. 650; Autocrates, Tympanistis. (p. 27)

[158] The wood was variously described, as beech, cedar, elm, ebony, grape. (p. 27)

[159] V. coins of Ephesus, Head, Hist. Num. (p. 27)

[160] On the Essenes cf. Paus. 8. 13, 1, where their rule of life is compared to that of the servitors of Artemis Hymnia at Orchomenus in Arcadia. The Talmud mentions a sect called Essenes, noted for their asceticism. (p. 27)

[161] Plut. An Sen. sit ger. Resp. p. 795D. The words are Μελλιέρη, Ἱέρη, Παριέρη. (p. 27)

[162] The word Megabyzus occurs frequently in Herodotus as a proper name among the Persians. Herod. 3. 70, 81, 82, 153, 160; 4. 43; 7. 82, 121. This is probably the basis of Farnell's statement (op. cit. 2. p. 481), that the use of the word at Ephesus points to Persian influence, which, according to Plutarch (Lys. 3) was strong here. Cf. Fairbanks, Greek Religion, App. 1. Strabo, p. 641. (p. 27)

[163] Paus. 7. 2, 7-8. (p. 27)

[164] Apart from the baetyl of Pessinus Cybele was regularly conceived as a beautiful matron. Cf. statue in Metroüm at Athens. For references v. supra, n. . (p. 28)

[165] Artem. Oneirocr. 2. 35. (p. 28)

[166] Paus. 7. 2, 8. (p. 28)

[167] Herod. 1. 171. The theory stated here is certainly that which Herodotus himself holds. He says that it was the Cretans' story that the Carians claimed to be autochthonous. Their tradition emphasised their kinship with the Lydians and Mysians. (p. 28)

[168] Herod. 1. 173. (p. 28)

[169] Paus, 7. 3, 7. (p. 28)

[170] The older name of Pamphylia was Mopsopia. Cf. stories of Mopsus, son of Cretan Rhacius, Paus. 7. 3, 2. Cf. Mela, 1; Plin. 5. 26. (p. 28)

[171] On the yearly feast of Artemis Pergaea and her mendicant priests, suggestive of those of Cybele, v. Parnell, op. cit. 2. p. 482. (p. 28)

[172] C. I. G. 6797. (p. 28)

[173] Soph. Oed. R. 204-208. (p. 28)

[174] Paus. 2. 31, 4-5. (p. 29)

[175] Ovid, Fasti, 3. 513. (p. 29)

[176] Cicero (Verr. 4. 48) uses Libera as the name of Proserpine. This doubtless is due to the close relation between Demeter and Dionysus. (p. 29)

[177] In addition to the passages already cited (Paus. 7. 2, 7-8; Tac. Ann. 3. 61) v. Plut. Quaest. Gr. 56. The story of Dionysus and the Amazons appears also in art. Cf. Arch. Ztg. 1845, pl. 30, showing sarcophagus from Cortona. (p. 29)

[178] Paus. 8. 23, 1. The chief temples of the place as described by Pausanias were of Artemis Ephesia, of Athena Alea, or Hippia (cf. Paus. 8. 47, 1), of Dionysus. Possibly the flagellation of women in the Dionysiac mysteries is represented on some frescoes recently

discovered in a Roman mansion near Pompeii (Nation, Dec. 1, 1910, p. 534). V. Am. Jour. Arch. 15 (1911), p. 567. (p. 29)

[179] Parnell believes that Ariadne was originally a Cretan goddess, who may easily have been identified with Cybele, Bendis, etc. (op. cit. 2. p. 473). Possibly the legend of Dionysus and Ariadne grew out of the Cretan cult in which he was her paredros. (p. 29)

[180] Aristot. Polit. 8. 7, 9; Eur. Bacch. 58. (p. 29)

[181] Herod. 4. 79; Athenaeus, 10. p. 445. (p. 29)

[182] Eur. Bacch. 821 ff. (p. 29)

[183] Aristid. Or. 4. p. 28; Aeschyl. Fr. Edoni ap. Aristoph. Thesm. 135. (p. 30)

[184] Apollod. 3. 5, 1. (p. 30)

[185] Cf. Atys as notha mulier, Catull. Atys, 27; Adonis, male and female, Orph. Hymn, 56. (p. 30)

[186] Plut. Thes. 23. On the rites of Ariadne-Aphrodite at Amathus v. Farnell, op. cit. 2. p. 634. Possibly some connection with Dionysus is implied in the strange epithet of Ephesian Artemis, Ἐλουσία, Hesych. s.v. (p. 30)

[187] Paus. l. c. (7. 2, 7-8); Tac. l. c. (3. 61). (p. 30)

[188] Ovid, Fasti, 2. 305 ff.; Apollod. 1. 9; 2. 7; Diod. Sic. 4; Prop. 3. 11, 17. (p. 30)

[189] V. supra, n. . (p. 30)

[190] The battle-axe receives special mention. Cf. double-axe of the Amazons. (p. 30)

[191] In a work now out of date (the Lydiaca of Th. Mencke, Berlin, 1843) there is valuable information on this subject. V. especially ch. 8. p. 22. (p. 30)

[192] The words of Tacitus (l. c.) representing the tradition at Ephesus itself, are very important: "Auctam hinc concessu Herculis, cum Lydia poteretur, caerimoniam templo." Heraclides Ponticus (Fr. 34), supposing Ἔφεσος and ἐφεῖναι to be etymologically akin, derives the name of the city from the attack which Heracles made on the Amazons from Mycale to Pitane. (p. 30)

[193] Paus. 3. 25, 1-3. Pausanias quotes Pindar on Silenus, "the zealous beater of the ground in the dance." (p. 32)

[194] Paus. 1. 41, 7. (p. 32)

[195] Iliad, 1. 38-39, and schol. ad l.; ibid. 451; Steph. Byz. s.v. Ἴλιον, Τένεδος; Paus. 10. 12, 1-6. Pausanias (l. c.) gives an account of the Sibyl Herophile, conceived to have been the second who filled the office at Delphi. The god whom she served was evidently identified with Smintheus. Herophile was called in some epic sources Artemis, in others, the wife of Apollo, in others, his daughter or a sister other than Artemis. She seems to have been in some way connected with Trojan Ida. (p. 33)

[196] Cicero, De Natura Deorum, 3. 57. (p. 33)

[197] Cf. Hoeck, Kreta, 3. p. 146. (p. 33)

[198] P. 36. (p. 33)

[199] Soph. l. c. (Oed. R. 204 ff.). The date of Sophocles in the best Greek period gives the passage special importance. (p. 33)

[200] Pind. Ol. 8. 47. (p. 34)

[201] Macr. Saturn. 1. 17-18. (p. 34)

[202] Farnell, op. cit. 2. p. 485. Elsewhere (2. p. 473) Farnell speaks of the identification between Artemis and the Semitic goddesses, Astarte, Derceto, Atargatis. (p. 34)

[203] Rouse, Greek Votive Offerings, p. 119. (p. 34)

[204] Paus. 4. 13, 1. (p. 35)

[205] Paus. 3. 16, 8. (p. 35)

[206] Paus. 3. 16, 7-9. (p. 35)

[207] Xen. Hell. 4. 2, 20. (p. 35)

[208] Pollux, 8. 91. (p. 35)

[209] Paus. 7. 26, 2-3. (p. 35)

[210] Paus. 4. 31, 8. (p. 35)

[211] Farnell (op. cit. 2. p. 471) suggests that Laphria is derived from λάφυρα. For a coin of Messene, which may represent Laphria, showing a woman huntress with a spear v. Imhoof-Blumer and Gardner, Numism. Comment. on Paus. p. 67, pl. P3. (p. 35)

[212] C. I. G. 2693. (p. 35)

[213] Le Bas, Îles, 2062. (p. 35)

[214] C. I. G. 3137. Cf. Tac. Ann. 3. 63. (p. 35)

[215] Paus. 8. 47, 6. (p. 36)

[216] Paus. 3. 14, 6. (p. 36)

[217] Cic. De Nat. Deor. 2. 27, 68; Paus. 1. 18, 5; 2. 22, 6-7; 7. 23, 5-7; 8. 21, 3. The Orphic Hymn to Artemis confuses her with Eileithyia and Hecate. (p. 36)

[218] On the Carnea, the chief festival of Sparta, v. Herod. 7. 206; 8. 72. This festival commemorated the Dorian conquest. Therefore during its celebration the people remained under arms and lived camp life. The feast was also one of harvest. Cf. the Jewish Feast of Tabernacles for a striking parallel. V. Mommsen, Heort. (p. 36)

[219] Paus. 3. 13, 3-5. (p. 36)

[220] Paus. 8. 24, 9. Apollo is called the patron of the Curetes against the Aetolians, Paus. 10. 31, 3. (p. 37)

[221] V. references in n. 217. (p. 37)

[222] Paus. 8. 37, 1. (p. 37)

[223] On the sanctuary of Despoena v. Paus. 8. 37, 1 ff. (p. 37)

[224] On the Titanes v. J. E. Harrison, British School Annual, 1908-09, pp. 308-338. (p. 37)

[225] Harrison and Verrall, Myth. and Mons. of Anc. Athens, p. 383. (p. 37)

[226] Ch. II, The Great Mother. (p. 38)

[227] Pollux, 8. 106. (p. 38)

[228] Paus. 9. 35, 1-7. The other Hora was Carpo. (p. 38)

[229] With Paus. 9. 35, 1-7 cf. Herod. 2. 50. Pausanias ascribes to Eteocles of Orchomenus the introduction of three Charites. Herodotus names the Charites among the aboriginal deities of the Hellenes. (p. 38)

[230] C. I. A. 4. 2, 1161 b; Lolling in Δελτ. Ἀρχ. 1891, pp. 25 ff., 126 ff.; Homolle in Bull. de Correspondance Hellén. 15 (1891), pp. 340 ff. (p. 38)

[231] C. I. A. 2. 741, Fr. a, 20; b, 14, 1207, 7; Judeich, Topographie v. Athen (Müller's Handb. d. klass. Altertumste. 3. 2, 2) p. 400. (p. 38)

[232] On the types of warlike Artemis v. supra, pp. 43-44. (p. 39)

[233] Paus. 7. 18, 11-13. (p. 39)

[234] For references v. n. 118. (p. 39)

[235] Cf. Farnell op. cit. 2. pp. 474-475. (p. 40)

[236] V. n. n. 122, 205. (p. 40)

[237] Cic. De Nat. Deor. 3. 23, 59. (p. 40)

[238] Cf. Paus. 1. 14, 7; 3. 23, 1. V. infra, ch. V, Ares. (p. 41)

[239] Possibly there is some support for Farnell's hypothesis, that Astrateia is a corruption for Astarte, in the words of St. Stephen's sermon recording the apostasy of the Jews to the Syrian goddess: ἔστρεψεν δὲ ὁ Θεὸς καὶ παρέδωκεν αὐτοὺς λατρεύειν τῇ στρατιᾷ τοῦ οὐρανοῦ, Acts, 7. 42. (p. 41)

[240] V. supra, pp. 45-46. (p. 41)

[241] Paus. 3. 18, 6-19, 5. V. Frazer's commentary on the passage. (p. 41)

[242] Paus. 3. 2, 6; 3. 19, 6. (p. 41)

[243] Paus. 3. 19, 6. There was a dispute between Amyclae and Mycenae, each of them claiming to possess the tomb of Cassandra (Paus. 2. 16, 6). The word Alexandra suggests the Trojan name of Paris. It implies a woman warrior, or one averse to marriage. In the latter connotation it

suggests Cassandra's refusal to marry Apollo after she had obtained from him the gift of prophecy; it suggests also the other famous story of the sacrilege of Ajax. (p. 41)

[244] Paus. 3. 26, 5. (p. 42)

[245] From the Agamemnon of Aeschylus it is to be inferred that the cult epithets of Trojan Apollo were Loxias and Agyieus, the names by which Cassandra cries to him. Loxias has the same significance, Eumen. 19. (p. 42)

[246] On the Hyacinthia v. Paus. 3. 19, 3-4; Athen. 4; Ovid, Met. 10. 219. In the Laconian myth Hyacinthus was the son of Amyclas, one of the autochthonous kings of Sparta. He became the favourite of Apollo, by whom he was accidentally slain. The legend presents parallels to the story of Agdistis and Atys and that of Aphrodite and Adonis. On the tale v. Paus. 3. 1, 3; 3. 10, 1. A legend of Salamis connected the origin of the hyacinth with the death of Ajax. (p. 42)

[247] Paus. l. c. (3. 25, 1-3). (p. 43)

[248] Paus. 3. 25, 1. (p. 43)

[249] Apollod. 1. 7, 6. (p. 43)

[250] Paus. S. 24, 9. It is interesting to compare the suggestion that the Cabiri were a primitive folk of Boeotia (Paus. 9. 25, 6). (p. 44)

[251] Il. 9. 527-599. Cf. Bacchylides, 5. 76-164. (p. 44)

[252] Paus, 10. 31, 3. (p. 44)

[253] Apollod. 1. 8, 2; Ovid, Met. S. 300; Hyg. Fab. 173. (p. 44)

[254] Iliad. 9. 557-560; Apollod. 1. 7, 9; Schol. Iliad (Ven.), 9. 553; Schol. Pind. Isth. 4. 92 (quoting Bacchylides). (p. 44)

[255] Iliad, 9. 565-572; Apollod. 1. 8, 1; Eurip. Meleager, Fr. 1. (p. 44)

[256] Schol. Ap. Rh. 1. 146. (p. 44)

[257] Paus. 3. 1, 1; 4. 1, 1. (p. 44)

[258] V. supra, ch. II, p. 23. Cf. Paus. 10. 38, 7. V. Toepffer, Attische Genealogie, p. 220. (p. 45)

[259] V. supra, ch. III, pp. 35 ff. (p. 45)

[260] Pind. ap. Paus. l. c. (3. 35, 2). (p. 45)

[261] Herod. 7. 26; 8. 138; Paus. 1. 4, 5; 2. 7, 9. (p. 45)

[262] Cic. De Nat. Deor. 3. 23, 58. (p. 45)

[263] Athenaeus (Deipnosoph. 14. 7) ascribes the invention of the Pyrrhic dance to Athena. Plato (Legg. 796 B) says that after the gigantomachy she imparted the rite to the Dioscuri. It is noteworthy that Melampus by a dance cures the Proetides whom Dionysus has driven mad (Apollod. 2. 3, 7), and that by some theologians Melampus was reckoned as a Dioscurus along with Alco and Tmolus, sons of Atreus (Cic. De Nat. Deor. 3. 21, 53). Dionysus himself was sometimes classed as a Dioscurus, i. e. at Athens in the worship of the Anaces (Cic. l. c.). (p. 45)

[264] Plut. Thes. 27. (p. 47)

[265] For Plutarch's version of the invasion (quoting Clidemus for details) v. Thes. 26-28. He finds it difficult to believe that a band of women could have conducted a campaign on the scale described in the current accounts, but finally accepts the fact. He doubts only the statement of Hellanicus, that they crossed the Cimmerian Bosphorus on the ice. (p. 47)

²⁶⁶ Plut. l. c.; Diod. Sic. 4. 28, 2, 3; Apollod. Epit. 1. 16; Aeschyl. Eum. 675 ff. (p. 47)

²⁶⁷ On the site v. Judeich, Topog. v. Athen, p. 269. (p. 47)

²⁶⁸ Aeschyl. Eum. 685-690. (p. 47)

²⁶⁹ The Greek is: πόλιν νεόπτολιν | τήνδ' ὑψίπυργον ἀντεπύργωσαν τότε, | Ἄρει δ' ἔθυον. It seems proper to contrast the imperfect ἔθυον with the aorist ἀντεπύργωσαν. (p. 47)

²⁷⁰ Plut. l. c. The verb is that employed of chthonic sacrifice, σφαγιάζω. On Phobus v. Iliad, 13. 299. (p. 47)

²⁷¹ Paus. 2. 32, 9. (p. 47)

²⁷² Cf. S. Wide, De Sacris Troezeniorum, Hermionensium, Epidauriorum, pp. 12 ff. (p. 48)

²⁷³ Frazer, Pausanias, 3. p. 281. (p. 48)

²⁷⁴ V. supra, ch. III, p. 38. For further references on the Oschophoria, v. J. E. Harrison, Prolegomena to the Study of Greek Religion, pp. 79 ff. (p. 48)

²⁷⁵ Paus. 2. 13, 3-4. (p. 49)

²⁷⁶ On this point v. Farnell, op. cit. 1. p. 200; 5. p. 126. (p. 49)

²⁷⁷ Paus. 8. 48, 4-5. (p. 49)

²⁷⁸ Paus. 8. 47, 2. (p. 49)

²⁷⁹ Paus. 8. 45, 5. (p. 49)

²⁸⁰ Paus. 8. 44, 7-8. (p. 50)

[281] On Dionysus Κρήσιος v. Paus. 2. 23, 7-8. (p. 50)

[282] Paus. 8. 45, 3. (p. 50)

[283] Paus. 8. 32, 3. The reference is to an altar of Ares said to be old. (p. 50)

[284] Paus. 8. 37, 12. The reference is to an altar of Ares in the temple of prophetic Pan above the shrine of Despoena. (p. 50)

[285] Arnob. Adv. Nat. 4. 25. (p. 50)

[286] Plut. Mulier. Virt. 5. Herodotus refers to the story, but not explicitly (3.76-83). Pausanias mentions the exploit, but does not speak of Ares (2.20, 8). (p. 50)

[287] Lactant. De Falsa Relig. 1. 20. Cf. Paus. 3. 17, 5. (p. 50)

[288] C. I. A. 2. 333; C. I. G. 3137; Fränkel, Inschr. v. Perg. 1. 13. (p. 50)

[289] Paus. 9. 4, 1. (p. 50)

[290] Paus. 1. 28, 5. (p. 50)

[291] In ancient literature the word Areopagus is always derived from Ares. (p. 51)

[292] Cf. Paus. 3. 23, 1; C. I. G. 3. p. 683, 1444; Antipater, A. A. O. 176. (p. 51)

[293] In the Aeschylean Septem the Thebans call upon Ares and Cypris as the ancestors of their race (125-129). (p. 51)

[294] On the marriage of Ares and Harmonia v. Hesiod, Theog. 933 ff. Cf. the stock genealogy in the Bacchae of Euripides. (p. 51)

[295] Tümpel, Ares u. Aphrodite, Fleckeisen's Jahrbücher, Suppl. 1 (1880), pp. 641-754. (p. 51)

[296] Arnobius, Adv. Nat. 4. 25. (p. 51)

[297] Paus. 3. 14, 10; 3. 20, 2. (p. 51)

[298] Rouse collects the examples, Greek Votive Offerings, p. 298, n. 9. (p. 52)

[299] Paus. 3. 19, 7-9. (p. 52)

[300] S. Wide, Lakonische Kulte, pp. 149 ff. (p. 52)

[301] British School Annual, 15 (1908-09), pp. 108-157; 16 (1909-10), pp. 4-11. (p. 52)

[302] Cf. Btsh. Sch. Annual, l. c.; Frazer, Paus. 2. pp. 358-359. (p. 52)

[303] Paus. 3. 19, 9. (p. 52)

[304] V. ch. IV, p. 55. (p. 52)

[305] Paus. 3, 15, 7. (p. 52)

[306] Paus. 3. 22, 7-8. (p. 52)

[307] Paus. 3. 15, 11. (p. 53)

[308] V. n. . (p. 53)

[309] Ascalaphus and Ialmenus of Orchomenus, sons of Ares by Astyoche: Iliad, 2. 511-515; 9. 82; 13. 518; Paus. 9. 37, 7. (p. 53)

[310] Phlegyas of Thessaly, son of Ares by Chryse of Orchomenus: Paus. 9. 36, 1-4. (p. 53)

[311] Evenus and Thestius, sons of Ares by Demonice: Apollod. 1. 7, 6. (p. 53)

[312] Meleager, son of Ares, rather than Oeneus, by Althaea: Apollod. 1. 8, 1; Eur. Meleager, Fr. 1. (p. 53)

[313] Paus. 1. 21, 4; Mar. Par., C. I. G. 2374, 5. (p. 53)

[314] Aëropus of Tegea, son of Ares by Aërope: v. supra, p. 60. (p. 53)

[315] Oenomaüs, reputed son of Ares by Harpina: Paus. 5. 22, 6. (p. 53)

[316] Melanippus, oecist of Tritea, son of Ares: Paus. 7. 22, 8. There was a Theban Melanippus, famous as a warrior at the time of the first attack on Thebes (Paus. 9.18, 1). There was also a Melanippus at Patrae in Achaea, who with his love Comaetho was sacrificed to Artemis Triclaria (Paus. 7. 19, 2-5). (p. 53)

[317] Farnell, op. cit. 2. p. 623. (p. 54)

[318] Odyssey, 11. 262. 6 (p. 54)

[319] Paus. 5. 15, 6. (p. 54)

[320] Hesychius s.v. (p. 54)

[321] Cf. Paus. 5. 13, 7. (p. 54)

[322] The name Pelops first appears in the Cypria (Schol. Pind. Nem. 10. 114). (p. 54)

[323] V. supra, p. 59. (p. 54)

[324] V. supra, n. . (p. 54)

[325] V. supra, ch. IV, p. 47. (p. 55)

³²⁶ Judeich, op. cit. p. 311. (p. 55)

³²⁷ Aeschyl. l. c. (Eum. 685-690). (p. 55)

³²⁸ Tümpel (op. cit.) finds traces of the Theban cult of Ares and Aphrodite in Attica. He does not take into consideration the connections of the legend of Ariadne. (p. 55)

³²⁹ Iliad, 5. 592. (p. 55)

³³⁰ V. supra, ch. II, p. 27, n. (p. 55)

³³¹ The early folk of Chalcis in Euboea seem to have been akin to the Leleges and Abantes of Boeotia. There were connections also with Chalcis of the Curetes in Aetolia. Cf. Iliad, 2. 536 ff.; Paus. 5. 22, 3-4; 9. 5, 1; 10. 35, 5. The most important connection here is that with Boeotia, where the worship of Ares certainly belonged. It is a curious fact that Chalcodon, the great Homeric hero of Euboea (Iliad, 2. 541), had an heroüm at Athens in the plain where there were many memorials of the Amazons (Plut. Thes. 27, 3). (p. 56)

³³² The genealogies of Thessaly are worth considering, because they show the persistent tradition of relationship between the primitive folk of this canton and Boeotia. V. n. . (p. 56)

³³³ Eur. Herc. Fur. Fr. 413. (p. 56)

³³⁴ Val. Flacc. 5. 90. (p. 56)

³³⁵ For references v. n. . (p. 56)

³³⁶ Ap. Rh. 2. 389; Schol. Tzetz. Post-Hom. 8. 189; Schol. Ap. Rh. 2. 1032; Hyg. Fab. 30, 112, 163, 223, 225. (p. 56)

³³⁷ The word appears in Pherecydes, but, because the corruption may be a scribe's error, no argument can be based on this. (p. 56)

[338] V. ch. I, p. 3. (p. 56)

[339] Herod. 5. 7. (p. 57)

[340] V. supra, pp. 26, 63. (p. 57)

[341] Among them are Miss Harrison (Proleg. pp. 375-379); Tümpel (op. cit. p. 662); Farnell (op. cit. ch. on Ares), who states the theory tentatively. (p. 57)

[342] Sophocles held this view (ap. Arnob. Adv. Nat. l. c.). Cf. St. Basil, who gives Ἀρεία as the old name of Thrace (s.v. Ἀρεία). (p. 57)

[343] J. E. Harrison, Proleg. l. c. (p. 57)

[344] Arnob. l. c. (Adv. Nat. 4. 25). (p. 57)

[345] V. supra, n. . (p. 57)

[346] Ap. Rh. 2. 1179; cf. 2. 387. V. supra, n. . (p. 57)

[347] Aristoph. Lys. 191. Undue importance has been given to the scholium by Preller-Robert (p. 343, n. 5), but, on the other hand, Farnell, in bringing forward this criticism, fails to give due weight to the quotation from Apollonius. (p. 57)

[348] V. supra, nn. , . (p. 58)

[349] Paus. 1. 21, 4; 1. 28, 5. (p. 58)

[350] Paus. 5. 15, 6. (p. 58)

[351] Harrison and Verrall, Myth. and Mons. p. 601. (p. 58)

[352] Arnob. Adv. Nat. 4. 25. On Scythian Ares cf. Herod. 4. 62. (p. 58)

[353] Cf. sacrifice of horses in Scythian tumuli, Arch. Anz. 1910, 195-244. (p. 58)

[354] Warde Fowler, Lustratio, pp. 186 ff. (p. 58)

[355] Warde Fowler, op. cit. and J. E. Harrison, Btsh. Sch. Annual, 1908-09, pp. 331 ff. (p. 58)

[356] Schol. Eur. Phoen. 1186. (p. 59)

[357] J. E. Harrison, Btsh. Sch. Ann. l. c. On chthonic Ares cf. Artemid. Oneirocr. 2. 34. (p. 59)

[358] Arnobius, l. c. (Adv. Nat. 4. 25). (p. 59)

[359] On the theory v. O. Klügmann, Philologus, 30 (1870), pp. 524-556. Stoll inclines to this theory, as shown by his article in Pauly's Realenc. s.v. Klügmann. Other advocates are Fréret, Mémoire de l'acad. d'inscr. 21. pp. 106 ff.; Welcker, Ep. Cycl. 2. pp. 200 ff. It is sympathetically treated in Roscher's Lexikon, s.v. Amazonen. Farnell seems inclined to accept it, although he does not explicitly advance an opinion. In one part of his work (op. cit. 5. p. 406) he takes the negative position that "the Amazon tradition is sporadic in Greece and perplexes the ethnographer and the student of religion," yet elsewhere (2. p. 482) he makes the close connection between Ephesian Artemis and the Amazons the basis of the suggestion that northern Asia Minor was perhaps the home of the cult. (p. 61)

[360] A. H. Sayce is the chief advocate of the importance of the Hittite kingdom. His most recent remarks on the Amazons are in Proc. Soc. Bibl. Arch. 1910, pp. 25-26. They are supported by A. J. Reinach, Rev. Arch. 1910, pp. 280-282. Cf. Leonhard, Hettiter u. Amazonen, 1911. (p. 61)

[361] This objection is made by Farnell, op. cit. 5. p. 406. (p. 61)

[362] This is the theory of Myres in Anthropology and the Classics, pp. 138 ff. Farnell is more satisfied with this than with the hieroduli theory (op. cit. 5. p. 406). (p. 61)

[363] Paus. 1. 23, 4. (p. 61)

[364] Cf. Myres, op. cit. pp. 153 ff. (p. 62)

[365] Paus. 5. 16, 1 ff. (p. 62)

[366] Apollod. 1. 9, 3. At Lemnos there were Corybantic rites of Bendis (Strabo, p. 466). (p. 62)

[367] The germ of the thought is in R. Y. Tyrrell's Preface to his edition of the Bacchae of Euripides. V. p. LXXXIII (ed. 1906) (p. 62)

www.ingramcontent.com/pod-product-compliance
Lightning Source LLC
Chambersburg PA
CBHW051606010526
44119CB00056B/800